APL: Equal Opportunities for All?

This book explores practical ways of implementing Accreditation of Prior Learning (APL) for the benefit of individuals, employers and the community as a whole. It shows how APL can make a real contribution to equality of opportunity.

Chapters consider the particular needs of various sectors of the community, and how APL can be used to meet those needs. For ethnic communities, those whose first language is not English, and those who arrive in Britain with qualifications from overseas, the APL process can be a vital stage in the search for education, employment and equality of experience. For people with disabilities APL can break through barriers and offer new breadth of opportunity. For women, often disadvantaged in the workplace, it can lead to recognition and improved career progression.

Through the use of case studies and practical examples, the authors offer detailed guidance on methods of implementation, staff development and continuing support to help tutors, managers and senior staff make effective use of APL systems.

Cecilia McKelvey is a Lecturer at Newham Community College. **Helen Peters** is Women's Development Officer at London Guildhall University.

D1334009

000085722

Further education: the assessment and accreditation
of prior learning series
Edited by Norman Evans and Michèle Bailleux, both
of the Learning from Experience Trust

Also available in this series:

Introducing APEL
Maggie Challis

APL: Developing More Flexible Colleges
Michael Field

APL: Equal Opportunities for All?

Cecilia McKelvey and Helen Peters

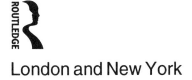

London and New York

First published in 1993
by Routledge
11 New Fetter Lane, London EC4P 4EE

© 1993 Cecilia McKelvey and Helen Peters

Typeset in Palatino
by LaserScript Limited, Mitcham, Surrey
Printed and bound in Great Britain by
Biddles Ltd, Guildford and King's Lynn

British Library Cataloguing in Publication Data

A catalogue record for this book is available from the British Library.

ISBN 0-415-09016-4

In memory of John Baillie,
Principal of Newham Community College (1985–91),
and Zara McKelvey

Contents

Foreword to APL: Equal Opportunities for All?

This book puts APL and APEL in the context of service to the whole community. Since the mid-1980s, when access to further and higher education became a focus for concern, the issues have widened to include those which Helen Peters and Cecilia McKelvey explore, and several factors have added to that concern. The economy, training and re-training needs, the growth in the number of refugees and other newly arrived immigrants, shifts of emphasis in government policy, including its determination to increase participation levels in both further and higher education, all bring to the fore questions of equity for all members of the community. For further education colleges this is happening in a dramatic way.

Incorporation thrusts colleges into a different relationship with the communities they serve. Working with Further Education Funding Council funding arrangements means providing access and equal opportunities for a range of disadvantaged groups differently, and more cost effectively. It represents a considerable challenge to all practitioners, whose experience of working with these groups indicates that the requirement is for intensive individual methods. Equal opportunities for women, for different ethnic communities, for speakers of other languages and dialects, for people with disabilities, become an institutional responsibility in a different way.

Drawing on their own practical experience, the authors of this book attempt to show how APL and APEL can be used to promote services for those groups of the population. They hope that by offering suggestions and examples of successful practice, they are making a contribution to the effort to improve them. The book is intended to be useful for practitioners, as well as those responsible for determining college mission statements and then finding ways of translating them into day-to-day action.

Norman Evans, Director, Learning from Experience Trust
Michèle Bailleux, Deputy Director, Learning from
Experience Trust
London, 1993

Foreword to the series

In Britain, the assessment and accreditation of prior learning (APL) began with the assessment of prior experiential learning (APEL). When discussion first began about APEL and further education, accreditation of anything other than examined outcomes was hardly on the map. Partly this was because APEL was seen as an additional way of widening access. But also it was because self-assessment stood out as one of the richest dividends for individuals from APEL. Accreditation might follow, but that was a separate issue. Over time, and that means from the early 1980s, the term APL has come to refer to all previously acquired learning, which necessarily includes experiential learning. So whereas APEL refers specifically to uncertificated learning, APL refers both to that and to previous learning that has been formally certificated through some recognised examining body. Both are vital. So often the one can lead to the other and both can serve as approach routes to additional formal learning. Throughout the books in this series, this distinction needs to be borne in mind. Perhaps the easiest way is to think of APEL as a subset of APL. And now, of course, accreditation is a lively issue for both.

Discussions about introducing the assessment of prior experiential learning to formal education in Britain began with higher education in the early 1980s. About two years later, further education entered the arena in two ways. Jack Mansell, then Chief Officer of the Further Education Unit, commissioned a project which resulted in the publication in 1984 of *Curriculum Opportunity: a map of experiential learning in entry requirements to higher and further education award-bearing courses*. Alun Davies, then the Chief Inspector for Higher and Further Education in the Inner London Education Authority, recognised the potential of APEL for further education as an influence on curriculum reform, staff development and for assisting colleges to prepare for a future that was going to be different from the past and present. So he gave a brief to a succession of enthusiastic and energetic staff in the Curriculum Development Unit to promote APEL activities in colleges wherever they could.

As some staff moved on to other posts inside and outside London, APEL activities spread so that by the time the National Council for Vocational Qualifications was established in 1986, there were staff in a number of further education colleges who had gone some way towards developing schemes for APEL, some of them promoted by the FEU, some of them connected with REPLAN projects for the unemployed. The Unit for the Development of Adult and Continuing Education took a hand through its programme of work on Access. And as Open College Federations and Networks worked at ways of awarding official recognition to non-institutional, off-campus learning, so they added yet another strand to APEL activities. As the benefits of progression and credit accumulation began to be more widely appreciated, both APL and APEL became an increasingly important dimension to Access, while NCVQ gave a strong lead in that direction through its own version of Prior Learning Achievements.

Now colleges face a different and uncertain future. It seems that to remain effective as incorporated institutions, they have to find ways of supplementing their funding from the FEFC, while pursuing policies designed to increase and widen participation. That means evolving imaginative forms of collaboration with industry and commerce. It means finding viable ways of handling Vocational Qualifications. And it all poses difficult organisational issues for a college that sets out to meet that range of requirements. So APL and APEL have become deadly serious considerations, so much so that it would be hard work to walk into any college without finding people who were talking about both. And often at the heart of those discussions there is the tension between using both APL and APEL for personal development and as a component of liberal education and seeing them as part of the provision for Vocational Qualifications.

In the real world of day-to-day activity in colleges, however, there is more talk than action. This is not surprising. Incorporating APL as a mainstream activity rather then seeing it as something rather fancy at the margins, touches issues from the top to the bottom of any institution. Overall management, academic organisation, the curriculum, modes of learning, teaching styles and delivery, admissions, student guidance and support systems, assessment procedures, relations with awarding bodies and NCVQ and, more recently, with higher education through franchising and associated status, all come into the reckoning. And since, as the books in this series imply, flexibility needs to be the hallmark of successful colleges in the future, and the effective introduction of APL requires flexibility, the message is clear. Colleges need APL to be flexible, effectively. APL requires flexibility to be successful within an institution.

This series of books on Further Education: the Assessment and Accreditation of Prior Learning, is a contribution towards encouraging colleges to incorporate APL schemes as mainstream provision. Moreover, we hope that because each of these books is written by men and women who know what they are talking about from their direct professional experience in the theory and practice of APL and APEL, whatever the particular focus of their writing, they will be of practical help to colleges and college staff wishing to develop schemes of their own.

Norman Evans, Director, Learning from Experience Trust
Michèle Bailleux, Deputy Director, Learning from
Experience Trust
London, 1992

Acknowledgements

The authors would like to thank the following people for their personal help and contribution of material: Tony Fazaeli (NIACE), Margaret Andrews (Birkbeck College), Noyona Chanda (Language and Literacy Unit), Jenny Warmington (Bournville College), Josephine Hewitt and Pauline Fearon (Business Studies Department, Newham Community College), Sally Faraday and Jenny Orpwood (Disability Learning Support Team, Newham Community College), Paul Edwards (Newham Sixth Form College).

For permission to reproduce the materials in this volume, acknowledgement is due to the following sources: Chapter 2, City and Guilds Equal Opportunities Statement, reproduced with the permission of the City and Guilds of London Institute; NVQ Note on Access and Equal Opportunities, reproduced with the permission of the National Council for Vocational Qualifications; Chapter 4, NIACE/TEED Project on Crediting Competence for Black/Ethnic Minority Adults with Overseas Qualifications Experience, reproduced with the permission of the Controller of Her Majesty's Stationery Office; Recognition of Overseas Qualifications: Doctors and Professional Requalifications: Lawyers, reproduced with the permission of the World University Service (UK); Chapter 8, examples from the Work Based Learning project: Crown Copyright, reproduced with the permission of the Controller of Her Majesty's Stationery Office.

Abbreviations

ABC	Administrative, Business and Commercial Training Group
ALBSU	Adult Literacy and Basic Skills Unit
APA	Accreditation of Prior Achievement
APEL	Accreditation of Prior Experiential Learning
APL	Accreditation of Prior Learning/Assessment of Prior Learning
BCODP	British Council of Organisations of Disabled People
BTEC	Business and Technology Education Council
CATS	Credit Accumulation and Transfer Scheme
CGLI	City and Guilds of London Institute
CLAIT	Computer Literacy and Information Technology
CNAA	Council for National Academic Awards
DES	Department of Education and Science (now DfE – Department for Education)
ESOL	English for Speakers of Other Languages
FEU	Further Education Unit
GNVQs	General National Vocational Qualifications
LCC	London Chamber of Commerce
LSHAPE	Language Support for Higher Education Access Programme in East London
NARIC	National Academic Recognition Information Centre
NATECLA	National Association of Teachers of English and Community Languages to Adults
NCVQ	National Council for Vocational Qualifications
NELAF	North East London Access Federation
NIACE	National Institute of Adult Continuing Education

NNEB   National Nursery Examination Board
NVQs   National Vocational Qualifications
OQP   Overseas Qualified People
PLAB   Professional and Linguistic Assessment Board
RSA   Royal Society of Arts
TEED   Training, Enterprise and Education Directorate
TVEI   Technical and Vocational Education Initiative
UDACE   Unit for the Development of Adult Continuing
            Education
WUS   World University Service

Chapter 1

Introduction

WHAT IS APL?

APL, or Accreditation of Prior Learning, is the process of identifying, assessing and accrediting a person's competences, knowledge and skills, however they have been acquired. Where this concerns uncertificated learning it is known as the Assessment of Prior Experiential Learning (APEL) and is a subset of APL. It constitutes, essentially, a formal recognition of the fact that people learn many things and acquire many skills outside the formal structures of education and training.

The process that individuals go through for the purposes of APL is in itself of value in helping them to analyse and assess their previous experience, and develop a sense of individual worth and growth. It serves as an opportunity to explore learning and career needs and work out future directions. It may also lead to formal recognition of achievement in the form of National Qualifications, promotion for people who are already in work, acceptance on courses in higher education and sometimes credit towards other qualifications.

For employers APL offers the opportunity of recognising the skills and abilities of their employees for the purposes of promotion, identifying further training needs, and improving the utilisation of human resources.

For educational establishments, APL provides a means of matching provision much more closely to demand, and of attracting a broader spectrum of students who can start the educational process from the point most appropriate to them and achieve their aims by the most direct route.

Why APL?

In the European context, with only one in three workers in Britain holding a vocational qualification compared to 64 per cent and 40 per cent of the workforce respectively in Germany and France, for example, the need for assessment and accreditation both for those in work and those seeking employment is pressing.

The government currently spends over £2 billion on education and training for adults, soon to become the responsibility of the Further Education Council. Nearly two million students study in further education colleges, about 80 per cent of them part time. The 1991 White Paper *Education and Training for the 21st Century* emphasises the importance of good quality education for adults 'to help them improve their qualifications, update their skills and seek advancement in their present career or in a new career'. APL is an important means of attaining this goal

APL for the whole community

It is the aim of this volume to demonstrate ways in which APL can be implemented in order to offer greater opportunities for self-realisation to individuals from all sectors of the community, to improve the service offered to those seeking education and training, and to increase the overall numbers of people with recognised qualifications. The prime objective of APL is to broaden the range of those participating, and increase recognition of the different types of experience people have to offer.

In order to do this, we shall be looking at the different sectors of the population in terms of what qualifications they have, what types of employment they are involved in, the levels and areas of unemployment and who is affected. We shall be questioning the lack of recognition of skills and experience in particular sections of the population, and looking at ways of improving assessment and accreditation of competence for them.

The following facts and figures are drawn from *Social Trends*, a publication of the Government Statistical Service (Central Statistical Office 1992), in order to give an indication of areas where APL can have a particularly useful function, as a preamble to examining in detail the equal opportunities implications.

Qualifications

Since the introduction of GCSEs in 1988 the proportion of pupils leaving school with no graded examination result has fallen to 9 per cent of boys and 7 per cent of girls. However, the proportion of 16- to 18-year-olds participating in education and training in the UK, at 69 per cent, is one of the lowest in the European Community, with only Italy and Spain coming off worse. Looking solely at 16-year-olds, the UK had the lowest full-time participation rate (only 50 per cent) in 1988. So for a large proportion of young people, education ends at 16, at least temporarily, and they join the labour force, with few or no qualifications.

As far as the total population of working age is concerned, in 1992, 29 per cent of men and 36 per cent of women had no qualification at all. Figures for different ethnic groups show a greater proportion of both men and women from Pakistan and Bangladesh having no qualification, with the figure for men being 52 per cent and that for women 68 per cent.

Parents' socio-economic group also has a significant bearing on the level of qualification of their children, with 54 per cent of the children of unskilled manual workers being unqualified, 47 per cent of the children of semi-skilled workers and 37 per cent of those of skilled manual workers. These figures give us a picture of a significant proportion of the adult population whose skills and experience are going unrecognised and who could benefit from APL as a means towards qualifications.

Immigrants and asylum seekers

In the last half of the 1980s about 47,000 people were accepted for settlement in the UK, of which nearly half came from Asia, and another 16 per cent from Africa. In addition, between 1989 and 1991 the number of applications for asylum increased dramatically, with 57,000 in 1991, or one per thousand of the population, compared to 22,000 in 1990 and 10,000 in 1989. These new arrivals to the country bring with them a wealth of experience and often high-level qualifications from their country of origin or another country. Recognition of their existing skills through APL, together with advice and counselling, is essential, if they are to reorientate themselves towards building a new life and career in this country.

Employment

The labour force is undergoing changes which have significant implications for education and training, and call for flexible approaches. Between 1971 and 1990 the number of women in the labour force rose by three million, while the number of men rose by only 300,000. This trend is projected to continue to the extent that by the turn of the century women will make up 45 per cent of the total civilian labour force. The increase in the number of women working outside the home is partly due to an increase in the availability of part-time jobs but also relates to demographic factors such as comparatively low birth rates and a rise in the average age at which women have children. Women in the Pakistani and Bangladeshi communities, however, show a different trend, with only 24 per cent involved in economic activity outside the home. Women in all socio-economic and ethnic groups tend to stay out of employment while their children are very young, with 57 per cent of all mothers of under 5-year-olds not working outside the home, whereas 72 per cent of women with no dependent children are in employment.

At the same time the number of young people in the labour force is falling and is projected to continue to fall by a further 800,000 by the year 2001. The changing age structure of the labour force presents recruitment problems for employers. Those employers who rely on young people as a significant source of employees face declining numbers until the mid-1990s. They therefore need to make better use of alternative recruitment sources, such as the unemployed, women returners to the labour market and older workers.

Part-time employment

Of those who worked part time in 1990, 86 per cent were women. Many people work part time because they want to. Only 6 per cent, in the 1990 figures, worked part time because they could not find a full-time job. However, part-time workers frequently experience fewer benefits from training and development programmes at work and have poorer chances of promotion. APL offers opportunities for part timers to gain recognition of their achievements and extend their skills.

People with disabilities

Among those who work part time by choice, 2 per cent do so because they are ill or disabled. Of the six and a quarter million disabled people in Britain nearly 200,000 are currently pupils in hospital schools, special schools or other public sector schools. These young people preparing to enter the labour force, and those who are already working full time or part time, or who are unemployed, may have skills and abilities which are not recognised by traditional qualifications. Discrimination through attitudes to disabled people or through environmental barriers may have hindered their access to education and training, yet they may have acquired valuable skills and experience. APEL has a role to play in ensuring that those skills are recognised.

Self-employment

Self-employment has increased dramatically over the last decade. After changing little during the 1970s, the number of self-employed people increased by 57 per cent between 1981 and 1990, with almost half of them working in the construction sector or the distribution, catering and repairs sectors of the economy. Many people who are self-employed do not have formal qualifications, yet the skill and expertise they build up is considerable. APEL provides a means of quantifying and building on those skills.

Unemployment

The number of unemployed (using the claimant count) rose above two million in 1991 with unemployment rates being highest among the young, particularly those under 20. The Labour Force Survey, which is a household survey, gives an estimate a quarter higher than the claimant count, part of which would be accounted for by the fact that most married women stop signing on after one year of unemployment, because their entitlement to benefit comes to an end if their husband is working or claiming.

Some factors that influence unemployment duration are race, disability, age and previous occupation. Unemployment rates are higher among other ethnic groups than among white people, particularly for Pakistani and Bangladeshi men and women and

West Indian men, although the rate of unemployment is also falling more rapidly for those groups. According to Colin Barnes, research worker for the British Council of Organisations of Disabled People 'they (disabled people) are three times more likely to be out of work than their non-disabled counterparts, and three times more likely to be out of work for long periods' (Barnes 1992). The length of unemployment for all groups also increases with age, with 28 per cent of unemployed men aged between 50 and 59 having been unemployed for more than three years. Looking at previous occupation, in 1990, 41 per cent of unemployed people had previously been employed in manual occupations. There is also an apparent mismatch between the skills of unemployed people and those required by employers, coupled with problems in how unemployed people obtain information about jobs and apply for them. APL clearly has an important role to play in assessing the skills of unemployed people, accrediting them and enabling them to build on those skills as a means of entering an appropriate and satisfying occupation.

In terms of social trends, then, we are looking at a substantial level of unemployment, particularly amongst young people, certain ethnic groups and women. At the same time employers are having to rethink recruiting targets and prepare to take on a workforce of a different nature, including more older people and more women. Other important groups to consider in terms of skills and training are part-time workers (predominantly women), people with disabilities, self-employed people, and new arrivals to the country.

EQUALITY OF OPPORTUNITY

In the subsequent chapters of this book, we are going to focus on some of the groups mentioned above, to examine in greater detail how APEL can be implemented for the benefit of individuals, employers and the community as a whole. We will first of all look at issues relating to equality of opportunity. Legislation to prevent discrimination on racial grounds has been on the statute book for some time, as well as legislation aimed against discrimination against women, although many would question the effectiveness of such legislation. A bill has been proposed to prohibit discrimination against disabled people but has not yet become law. Many organisations have equal opportunities policies and many employers call themselves 'equal opportunity employers'. Certainly not many educational establishments or companies would admit to any kind of discrimination in their recruitment methods. Yet the statistics clearly indicate that sections of the population are at a disadvantage, both in employment terms and in relation to education and training.

In Chapter 2 we will look at the aims of some of these policies, and how they are put into practice. We will examine the equal opportunities policies and statements of bodies such as the National Council for Vocational Qualifications (NCVQ) and City and Guilds and at how practical implementation of policies can be provided for, on the grounds that the point at which a policy has a genuine effect is when the resources are made available to put practical procedures into place. We will suggest that APL is one practical procedure which can contribute enormously to the real implementation of equality of opportunity. Finally we will give a brief outline of the APL process and look at some of the implications for access to higher education within the context of Credit Accumulation and Transfer Schemes (CATS).

The different ethnic communities

In Chapter 3 we will look at some of the different ethnic communities in Britain, with the aim of highlighting what particular education and training needs are not being met and what role APL could play in meeting them. We will look first at the Afro-Caribbean communities and what factors have led to them being disadvantaged in the education system, such as the failure to acknowledge the validity of their different cultural background, and to recognise the complex language situation of people of Caribbean heritage. We will then look at some of the communities where other languages are spoken, what difficulties members of those communities experience in the education system and the job market, what areas of work they are involved in and what talents and skills are going unrecognised or being under utilised.

Recognition of qualifications from overseas

The first stage for many new arrivals, whether they have come to this country specifically for education or training or whether they have come to build a new life, is to establish the status of the qualifications they already have. The recognition of equivalences between qualifications can save precious time and money spent on repeating studies already started or completed elsewhere. Even partial recognition can give valuable credits towards full accreditation. Chapter 4 will outline ways in which recognition of overseas qualifications can be obtained through the British Council and report on the work of the National Institute of Adult Continuing Education (NIACE) in the area of crediting claimed competence for black adults with overseas qualifications. Some existing projects for helping people with qualifications and/or experience overseas will be discussed and some of the difficulties encountered by participants.

APL and speakers of other languages and dialects

A lack of knowledge of the English language is very often automatically considered a barrier to access to education, training and employment. Speakers of other languages, even with a fairly high level of English, are often referred to language classes without consideration of their other skills and/or qualifications. In Chapter 5 some practical proposals will be outlined for getting round the artificial barrier language poses for APEL. These will include strategies such as the use of interpreters and written translations. We will look at ways in which practical assessments can be conducted, where appropriate, in an environment where the use of language is not necessary, and at the possibility of training assessors who speak other languages, so that if people are working in an environment where their mother tongue is spoken, as is often the case, they can be assessed without recourse to English. Case studies will again be used to demonstrate these possibilities. The ability to speak more than one language needs to be recognised as a skill in itself, and strategies for raising language awareness among some of the bodies involved in accreditation will also be considered.

Practical implications of APL for people with disabilities

The range of possible types and degrees of disability is extremely broad and the practical implications for accreditation correspondingly so. We will start, in Chapter 6, by looking at physical disabilities. People who are deaf or hearing impaired, those who are blind or partially sighted, wheelchair users or people who have other physical disabilities, have as much if not more to offer in terms of skills and abilities, as many able bodied people. Nevertheless, the barriers posed by inaccessible buildings and facilities, lack of staff development and resources, and prejudice, mean that many talents and energies are unrecognised and wasted. Students with learning difficulties also face considerable barriers to traditional methods of education. Accreditation of competences may prove a rewarding process for them as a way to build positively on the skills they have, rather than being measured negatively against the achievements of those without difficulties. Some practical possibilities for APL for disabled people will be considered and a case study included as an example.

APL and women

We have already mentioned the fact that a higher percentage of women than men have no qualification, particularly among certain ethnic groups. We have also noted that the majority of women stay at home while their children are under school age, that the vast majority of part-time workers are women, and that the number of women in the labour force is rising fast. Far more men than women are in managerial and professional jobs. This suggests a large workforce of women who are underqualified and disadvantaged in the workplace, often because they have spent time at home bringing up children and have then gone into part-time work in order to maintain the home and family. There is now a growing awareness from validating bodies that most women bring to work and education a variety of skills and competences learned experientially outside institutions. Many women from all ethnic groups also have substantial experience of work in voluntary organisations. Probably more progress has already been made in the area of APL for women than in any of the other areas mentioned above. In Chapter 7 we will describe some of the work done on the accreditation of competence gained in unpaid work, and innovations such as the Advanced Diploma in the Organisation of Community Groups developed by the RSA to accredit experience gained through voluntary work. Again, practical examples of individual cases will be given.

Issues of class

In Chapter 8 we will look more closely at some of the issues relating to class differences which have arisen in preceding chapters. What are the barriers that prevent the majority of young people from continuing in education and training after the age of 16? Why do more people not take advantage of alternative routes into higher education? What role does APL have to play in this and how can it be used practically to encourage people of all ages to value their skills and abilities and build on them? These questions hinge on the relationship between the individual and society. We will look at some examples of ways in which change can be brought about, through shifts in the traditional view of education and the breaking down of the academic/vocational divide, and through initiatives such as APL for school students and Work Based Learning.

In the concluding chapter, the different strategies for the delivery of greater equality of opportunity through APL will be summed up, with the advantages they will offer to the different groups targeted. Finally, we will stress the importance of working closely with awarding bodies to ensure that they are fully aware of equal opportunities dimensions and implications, and the importance of ensuring involvement from the target groups at every level of the process, as assessors, verifiers and members of awarding bodies as well as candidates for APL. We have included some examples of practical exercises in most chapters in the hope that they will serve as a trigger to the development of APL procedures in a wide range of different contexts.

Chapter 2

Equality of opportunity and the APL process

The equal opportunities policies of the major examining and validating bodies are of course very similar to each other, and together reflect the concerns of educational institutions to provide 'access to all' regardless of age, gender, racial origin, religious persuasion, sexual orientation or disability. By this they mean essentially access to courses, examinations and assessment. The examining and validating bodies' equal opportunities statements express a determination to avoid the creation of inequalities through the format and content of regulations, examinations and other assessment material. City and Guilds of London Institute (CGLI) make a commitment to 'the relaxation of any conventional rules and regulations which serve to inhibit the performance of those candidates with special needs in relation to candidates not so disadvantaged, provided that such action does not have a deleterious effect on the standard, quality and integrity of the assessments' (CGLI 1992).

In other words the standard is set but the way in which a candidate can show how she or he meets the standard is flexible. This is also at the heart of the claim of NCVQ that it has improved access to qualifications and equality of opportunity for those traditionally more likely to be excluded by the system of vocational qualifications.

THE NATIONAL COUNCIL FOR VOCATIONAL QUALIFICATIONS (NCVQ)

The National Council was established in order to reform a chaotic system of vocational qualifications, with the primary objective of making them more accessible to individuals. As we mentioned in

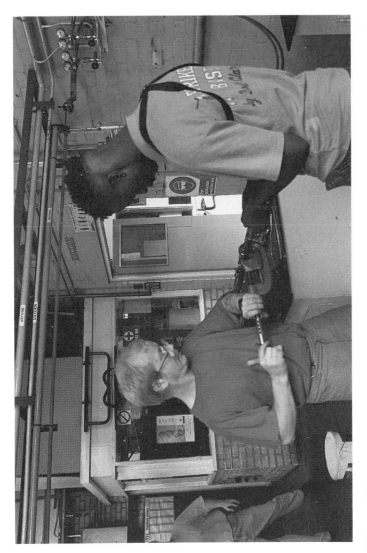

Chapter 1, the percentage of the workforce in the UK with vocational qualifications is very low compared to our major competitors abroad, and the emphasis that the NCVQ gives to equality of opportunity stems partly from the fear that the UK will be unable to compete well in the European Community, together with apprehension that demographic changes in the 1990s will lead to a drying up of the workforce, which will hamper economic performance. The NCVQ framework requires that awarding bodies ensure that nothing discriminatory is built into competence specifications or assignments. Some of the characteristics designed to remove barriers are:

1 Candidates must meet the standard and performance criteria for assessment. Language may not be relevant to the competence being demonstrated, for example, in catering. Assignments may be conducted in Welsh, Gaelic or any other indigenous language, subject to evidence that the candidate is competent in English to the standard required for employment in the UK.
2 No lower or upper age limits are stipulated except where imposed by law, such as for a driving licence or in the case of certain Health and Safety Regulations, for example, under 16-year-olds are not allowed to cut up meat.
3 No conditions are stipulated relating to the attainment of prior qualification, preparation over a specified period or having attended a course or a particular institution. However, if a candidate has not attended a course, assessor and candidate have no knowledge of each other, the shared vocabulary and experience are not there, and there can be no assumption of knowledge and skills.
4 APL is available to enable candidates to gain units or whole qualifications. Assessors have to remember that they are only awarding competence for each unit. Even if candidates are unsuitable for a whole qualification, if they show evidence that they reach the standard of competence outlined by the unit statement, that is sufficient for it to be awarded.
5 The extension of vocational qualifications into new areas such as Afro hairdressing or Chinese cookery may help people previously excluded from gaining qualifications.

The NCVQ framework is based upon elements and units of competence with related performance criteria which describe what is to be assessed and how. These statements have been identified as requirements of employment by the leading industry bodies. They are national and cannot be altered. However, the way in which competence is demonstrated and assessed may vary. Assessors are given the freedom to devise assessments and must be aware that 'the mode of assessment should not constitute an artificial barrier to gaining an award if performance in respect of that competence is not dependent on the one mode' (NCVQ 1988).

NVQs provide a framework for assessment and awards will reflect the quality of the assessment. If the assessment is inferior then the award will quickly become valueless. Assessors have more freedom in devising assessment tasks but greater constraints, in that they must ensure competence statements are met in accordance with performance criteria. They must neither under assess nor over assess. In order to do this they must free themselves of prejudice concerning the sorts of people likely to be successful, and concentrate on statements and performance criteria. On the other hand they must have a knowledge of the sort of experience likely to lead to competence in a given area, and must be able to suit the assessment not only to the statements but also to the candidates. They must be knowledgeable about different assessment methods and be flexible in their application. They must consider the uses of:

- product assessment
- performance or demonstration techniques
- the use of oral questioning
- simulation and written tasks.

APL candidates will come with large amounts of evidence of their achievements. The assessor must learn to evaluate this. Assessors must be trained to be aware of the various factors which could discriminate against candidates. For instance, if a candidate for a catering qualification cannot write very well the assessment could be conducted orally. Equally, the correct interpretation and use of the performance criteria is of crucial importance. Failure to relate the interpretation of performance criteria to the national framework could result in subjective assessments. For instance, candidates are competent at Level 1 if they can achieve competence criteria under supervision and in a restricted range of work conditions. This could have important implications for candidates with special needs. A person with a visual impairment, for example, might be able to carry out filing using braille tabs and be able to achieve competence at Business Administration Unit Level 1 for filing. However, she or he might not be able to achieve it at Level 11, which would require being able to work without supervision.

APL and NVCQ

APL is an integral part of the NCVQ framework and, together with the credit accumulation facility offered by NVQs, is regarded as the component most likely to attract those who have turned their backs on vocational qualifications before, or failed to achieve them through disadvantage. The NCVQ framework has enabled APL to be seen as part of a comprehensive range of national vocational awards. APL has rightly been seen as a powerful mechanism to enhance and develop access to learning opportunities, but people belonging to those groups traditionally disadvantaged by the educational system are aware of a number of potential barriers:

1 The leading industry bodies, made up of employers, devised the standards of competence, and employers have been accused of reproducing and reinforcing the old divisions in the labour market that are the basis of inequality. The standards set by these bodies and the academics in universities are not value free and arguably reinforce the status quo.
2 The focus in APL is on outcomes of learning that have taken place prior to assessment. The learning experiences are regarded merely as a means through which specific knowledge and skills were acquired. The context of the learning is therefore dismissed. For women and those with special needs this may be very damaging, particularly if experience fails to meet standards of competence.

The opening up of the world of unpaid work to assessment through the NCVQ system is potentially an important breakthrough in giving value to the vast number of people, estimated at six million, who are occupied full time in unpaid work. By defining work as 'purposeful activity with critical outcomes' (NCVQ 1988) the NCVQ and most of the awarding bodies have opened up the prospect of gaining vocational qualifications through APL for those involved in unpaid work. However, it is important to realise that the particular criteria, developed by industry, often preclude the inclusion of experience acquired in a non-commercial context. On the other hand, particular quali-fications such as the RSA Diploma in the Organisation of Community Groups have been developed for those who work in a voluntary capacity. Nevertheless, where any transfer of the competence of women or people with disabilities is made into paid employment it is usually into low-quality and low-level work. It is important that those involved should move on and not simply have their place in society confirmed by a system which merely matches competences acquired in a domestic context to Level 1 qualifications.

Before looking at particular issues in further detail it would be valuable to go through the APL process. Although it is not our intention to describe the basic details, it is important to develop some appreciation of what the process involves. Here the NCVQ model is first described.

Outline of the process

Prior learning achievement refers to the totality of what someone knows, understands and can do at the time of assessment for a qualification. This covers achievements both from formal study and those acquired through experience. In order to obtain credit for achievements the evidence must be matched to the assess-ment requirements for a particular NVQ or unit of credit. In this way a computer programmer might wish to present evidence consisting of a portfolio of programs produced in the course of a job. A caterer may be able to produce menus and costings of products from working in the industry. Evidence may come from:

• courses for which certification is available stating what was achieved
• employment and unpaid voluntary work
• independent study, e.g. correspondence courses, distance learning or in-company training
• life experiences.

The NVQ model is particularly suited to APL. The statement of competence describes the standard to be reached independently of any training or education programme. The related perform-ance criteria define how it is to be assessed. The division of

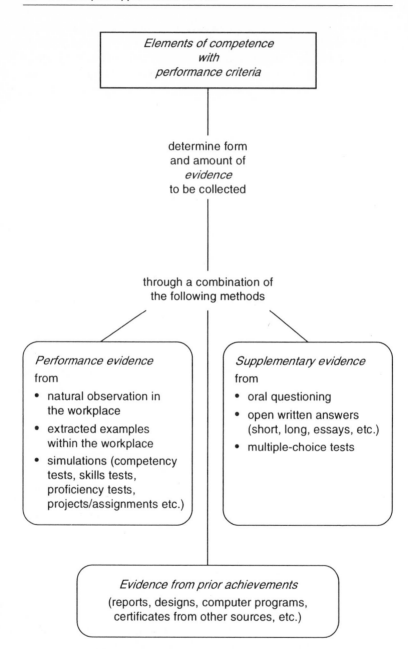

Figure 2.1 NVQ assessment model

qualifications into units which can be accredited separately means that candidates have a better chance of gaining unit credits through APL. To gain credit for a particular unit, evidence must be produced. Evidence can be from past achievements, current assessment or a combination of both. Potential sources of evidence are:

- written reports: articles, designs, accounts using specialised language
- previous certification or records of achievement
- products or artefacts
- testimonials endorsed by an employer.

These can be supplemented by current assessment such as oral or written questions, assignments or performance testing. The evidence produced must match each of the performance criteria for the element of competence being claimed. If someone with previous office experience involving clerical or receptionist duties recognised their experience as relevant to filing, for example, they would have to show how their achievement related to the following competences and their criteria:

- File documents and open new files within established filing, requires the following performance criteria:
  - document filed in correct location and sequence in system
  - materials stored in safe manner
  - records up to date and accurate
  - all documents classified correctly.
- Identify and retrieve document within established filing system.

The APL process entails a number of stages and candidates are given guidance as to what qualifications might be suitable.

Stage 1   The candidate recognises experience which is likely to link up with the qualification.

Stage 2   The candidate identifies and records achievement.

Stage 3   Evidence is assembled and organised into a portfolio to suit the regulations of particular awarding bodies.

Stage 4   The candidate submits evidence of achievement via the portfolio to the assessor.

Stage 5   The candidate meets the assessor and may undergo a skills test, interview or simulation.

Stage 6   The assessor evaluates the evidence and the candidate receives verification from the awarding body.

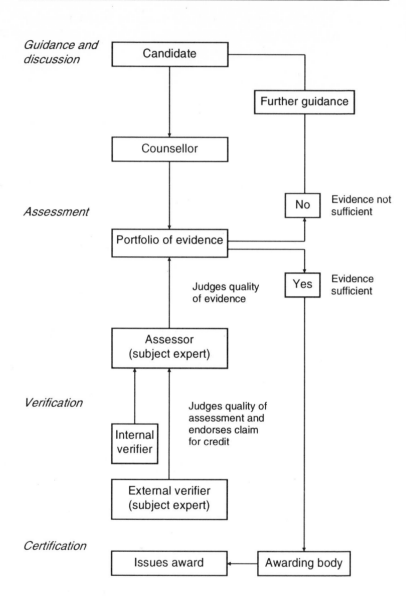

Figure 2.2 The APL process

Stage 7 The candidate receives information on learning opportunities.

Four people are usually involved in this process:

- The candidate, who is responsible for

  - identifying the NVQ with the advocate
  - assembling and providing evidence to support the APL claim.

- The counsellor/advocate, who is responsible for

  - assisting the candidate to identify the target NVQ
  - preparing an action plan of the units needed to gain the qualification or the units to be attempted
  - scrutinising the candidate's previous experience and qualifications to see whether an APL claim is possible
  - helping the candidate identify sources of evidence
  - helping the candidate compile the evidence
  - arranging assessment
  - undertaking all administrative work in connection with the candidate's claim
  - discussing the assessor's verdict and agreeing further action.

- The assessor, who is responsible for

  - assessing, as subject expert, direct and indirect evidence of the candidate's achievement
  - interviewing the candidate
  - submitting a report on the claim
  - providing information to the Examining and Validating Body verifier.

- The verifier, who is responsible for

  - ensuring the assessment procedures are in accordance with NVQ principles
  - giving advice to APL staff
  - reporting to the awarding body on APL procedure.

We next give some examples of assessment techniques, list types of evidence and look at some key points in validation.

PROVIDING EVIDENCE OF PRIOR LEARNING

Possible assessment techniques

1 Situational observation: observation of student's performance in a real situation and attesting demonstration of competence, for example, at work, in voluntary activities, at public meetings.
2 Performance testing: a more controlled version of situational observation involving performing some competence(s) either in a real-life situation or in one devised in a testing station. An example would be an arranged conversation with a French speaker who could attest a student's competence in spoken French.
3 Simulation or role play: a special situation devised to allow performance testing to take place. It is useful for demonstrating competences in the inter-personal sphere which are difficult to isolate.
4 Product assessment: a method of substantiating competence(s) by presenting a product in which they are embodied, for example producing a table, a picture, a photograph.
5 Written assignments: the portfolio autobiography is a large written assignment and should contain all the evidence about what a student knows and can do. Further evidence can be provided through written assignments under controlled classroom conditions.
6 Examinations and tests: tests of knowledge, whether essay-type, multi-choice or simple questions could be used to support evidence from real life tests or where these were taken some time ago and there is doubt as to their currency.
7 Oral interview: this could be used to provide evidence of particular competences in verbal presentation, or simply as question-and-answer to test students' knowledge.

Evidence

Evidence may fall into three broad categories: existing certificated learning; prior learning achievement for which evidence is readily available; prior learning achievement claimed or identified, but for which there is no direct evidence.

1 Existing certificated learning: certificates issued by recognised examining bodies are, where appropriate, used to grant entry or exemption only. Other certificates, licences or test results

may provide evidence of skills or competence and may, subject to evaluation, be used for the award of credit.

2 Prior learning achievement for which evidence is readily available: examples of materials within this category are:

   (a) testimonials or other authenticated reports of achievements acquired in the past. Many testimonials submitted for evaluation are very general, and in consequence of little value. Specifically solicited testimonials, addressing clearly identified competences or skills are preferred;

   (b) presentation of products which demonstrate achievement, such as written or published material, computer programs, designs, objects, artefacts, etc.

3 Prior learning achievement which is claimed, but for which there is no direct evidence: the bulk of prior learning achievement will probably come within this category. A student will need guidance to reflect upon and set down relevant experiences in a structured manner, in order that claimed skills or competences can be identified and assessed. The significance of the term 'relevant' will depend upon the units for which credit or exemption is sought, but sources of prior learning achievement might include:

   (a) experience gained in the workplace;

   (b) informal or non-credit-bearing courses such as in-company training schemes or adult education;

   (c) independent and self-directed study, correspondence courses;

   (d) experiences such as voluntary work.

Key points in the validation of evidence

How do you know the candidate's claims are genuine?

• Observation is indisputable – many other forms of evidence are not.

• Written assignments could be written by anyone unless they are done in your presence. They therefore require questioning.

• Product assessment requires probing questions from a qualified assessor to ensure that the product has been produced by the candidate.

• Letters of validation can, if properly constructed, be very useful but should always be questioned and verified if any doubts arise during questioning.

Currency of evidence

Has the candidate kept up-to-date with recent developments?

- Evidence from the distant past will not always prove competence and it is up to the assessor to ascertain that evidence proves what is intended.

Acceptability of evidence

Does the evidence match in part or wholly the competences set down in the performance criteria?

- Can it be believed?
- Has it been questioned?
- Has it been validated?
- Is it reliable?
- Is it practicable?

Sufficiency of evidence

- Does it cover *all* the performance criteria?
- Does it allow *all* the criteria to be met?
- Would you be happy to sit down with a subject assessor and justify the evidence for the portfolio?

If all of the above conditions have been met, then the evidence should conclusively prove competence or knowledge.

APL AND HIGHER EDUCATION

The influence of the United States has led to the development of APL in higher education in the UK, and the Council for National Academic Awards (CNAA) Regulations state that: 'A student's programme of study . . . may incorporate credit for appropriate prior learning and for the successful completion of employment based training' (CNAA 1989).

However, this has developed in a different way from NVQs. NCVQ and the Examining and Validating Bodies require that an individual's prior learning be matched to the standards of competence and performance criteria, whereas the CNAA guidelines define different sorts of credit:

1 General credit, which is not related to a particular course but is recognised as being of academic value at a given level, e.g. for communication skills or the ability to organise facts. This is then given a credit rating.
2 Specific credit, which is awarded towards the attainment of a specific programme. This credit should be related to the broad educational aims of the course, which should be stated in objective terms. The maximum number of credits will vary according to the award, e.g. up to sixty credits for a certificate, 240 for a degree.

The CNAA identify four stages to the APL process:

• identification of learning
• statement
• collection of evidence
• assessment.

Assessment can be through written evidence, interview, additional assignments, examination of projects, performance or an APEL module. As in the NCVQ model a mentor is identified, who acts as a guide in the preparation of the submission. The mentor is responsible for helping the student to prepare the submission and for suggesting evidence and methods of presentation.

The academic assessor has subject expertise in the area of the submission. The role of the assessor is to examine documentation and evidence and to interview the student with a view to establishing that academic learning has taken place as a result of experience. The assessor must take into account the candidate's level of academic knowledge and judge whether they have degree level skills. The assessor then reports to the assessment board to determine the level of specific credit.

The APL scheme fits into the Credit Accumulation and Transfer Scheme, in which credit can be given for previous formal courses of study or learning gained by experience. A block of study or a course unit is given a credit rating. Students undertake a programme of study which has stated aims and objectives and demonstrates coherence. This can be taken at more than one institution and may involve professional bodies and employment-based training centres. Each course unit is graded according to the quality of performance at assessment. Units passed are listed on a certificate of credit. The scheme clearly has the potential to open up new routes to higher education and to put it within the grasp of a broader section of the population, since if credit is awarded for learning from experience, for example, mature students can save valuable time and expense. Similarly those who have gained non-academic qualifications or who have qualifications from overseas can build on them rather than having to start at square one. Nevertheless, as in the NVQ context, change is obviously going to depend on the quality and adaptability of assessment, which in turn will depend on the training and ability of assessors and mentors.

In conclusion, the Examining and Validating Bodies and the CNAA have established principles which can be immensely useful in creating real equality of opportunity, if in practice those that implement those policies – colleges, assessors, counsellors – establish procedures and systems which show an awareness of the barriers which operate against people obtaining qualifications. APL is an opportunity, but the fact that it is theoretically possible for people to gain qualifications in this way does not necessarily mean that they will. The barriers will be different but they will still be there. Points to consider are:

1 How will people know about APL? How will it be marketed?
2 What sort of advice and counselling will candidates receive?
3 How much will it cost?
4 How will assessors and advocates be trained?
5 What qualifications will be offered?
6 What kind of advice, resources and support will be available?

We suggest that as a starting-point for initiating APL in an institution, interested staff can be asked to participate in a brainstorming session in small groups, in which they list the possible benefits to students and to the institution of providing a system of APL. Answers that came up in one staff development session included exemptions, assessment on demand, accreditation, an increase of self-worth for individuals, greater awareness of employment pathways, easier and quicker progression, enhanced learner motivation, savings and/or better use of resources, access to courses, greater equality of opportunity.

In the light of the stated aim of APL to open up greater

opportunities for accreditation and create a more qualified workforce, in subsequent chapters we will look at some of the individuals and groups that could benefit particularly from the process outlined above. We will discuss some of the difficulties and variables that could come into play and what solutions might be possible, and in so doing we will attempt to set APL in a real context, with case studies to illustrate actual results, and some practical suggestions for implementation of the process.

We conclude this chapter with the City and Guilds Equal Opportunities Statement and an NVQ Note on Access and Equal Opportunities, so that they can be used as reference points when looking at some of the issues around equal opportunities that come up in the following chapters.

CITY AND GUILDS EQUAL OPPORTUNITIES STATEMENT

1 This paper sets out City and Guilds' general policy with regard to equal opportunities.

2 As a national examining and awarding body, City and Guilds is responsible for ensuring that all candidates entered for assessment under the provision of its schemes are treated fairly and on an equal basis.

3 City and Guilds insists that there be open access by all providing bodies to its schemes and that the assessment of the performance of those entered shall ensure, wherever feasible, equality of opportunity regardless of a candidate's gender, age, racial origin, religious persuasion, sexual orientation or disability.

4 City and Guilds will ensure avoidance of inequality

- in the selection, recruitment and training of all those working for or on behalf of the Institute
- in the format and content of all syllabuses, regulations, examinations and assessment materials
- through the monitoring of practices, procedures and data relating to the operations of its schemes and assessment materials by approved centres
- in the preparation, production and distribution of all material by the Institute

- by the relaxation of any conventional rules and regulations which serve to inhibit the performance of those candidates with special needs in relation to candidates not so disadvantaged, provided that such action does not have a deleterious effect on the standard, quality and integrity of the assessments.

5 In formulating its schemes and assessment techniques, in operating its procedures and in producing its materials, City and Guilds will seek to ensure that for its part every reasonable effort is made to avoid a format, language or approach which, in relation to a candidate's gender, age, racial origin, religious persuasion, sexual orientation or disability

- is offensive to members of particular groups
- is not capable of being readily understood by some candidates
- does not have the same meaning for all candidates
- implies stereotyped or biased attitudes
- assumes experiences which not all candidates have had
- describes contexts which are not equally meaningful to all candidates
- includes terms or concepts or forms of presentation which are unfamiliar to some groups of candidates
- employs techniques that are easier for some groups of candidates to use
- requires activities which cannot be performed by all candidates.

6 In furtherance of this policy, City and Guilds will work in co-operation with all appropriate national and local organisations and agencies to develop means of identifying and preventing unequal opportunity in relation to assessment materials and procedures and in centre recruitment to City and Guilds schemes.

7 City and Guilds fully supports the principles of equal opportunities and is committed to satisfying these principles in all its activities and in its published material.

NVQ NOTE ON ACCESS AND EQUAL OPPORTUNITIES

This guide sets out NCVQ policy on access to qualifications in the context of equal opportunities. Open access through flexibility in assessment and learning has been deliberately incorporated into the design of NVQs to increase equality of opportunity and encourage more people to participate in education and training.

Outlined here are the practical ways in which the NVQ system promotes access to qualifications to give everyone the chance to develop and to have their achievements recognised within the national qualifications system.

NCVQ policy

Equal opportunities and open access are explicitly and implicitly embodied in the Council's criteria for the acceptance of a qualification as an NVQ.

The Council requires that all NVQs be:

- free from barriers which restrict access and progression, and available to all those who are able to achieve the required standard by whatever means
- free from overt or covert discriminatory practices with regard to gender, race and creed, and designed to pay due regard to the special needs of individuals
- based on assessments of the outcomes of learning, arrived at independently of any particular mode, duration or location of learning
- awarded on the basis of valid and reliable assessments made in such a way as to ensure that performance to the national standards can be achieved at work.

Open access to assessment

NCVQ requires that those bodies awarding NVQs promote access to assessment, including assessment for those who are not in full-time or paid employment, or for those in categories of employment that might restrict access to assessment.

The Council states that NVQs be free from age restrictions (unless required by law); that arrangements be made for assessing candidates with special needs, defined as including people with physical or sensory disabilities or learning difficulties, who may require support to undertake assessment. Such support could include physical, mechanical or technical aids, extra time for assessment, or specially devised or adapted methods of assessment.

The awarding bodies

NCVQ requires awarding bodies to have an equal opportunities policy, and a means of monitoring its implementation. The policy must be clearly communicated to candidates and organisations involved in the operation of the award. NCVQ's role is to assist awarding bodies in developing policies and practices that promote equal opportunities in NVQ delivery through their centres.

Awarding bodies are encouraged to develop their equal opportunities practices further with regard to:

- the communication and marketing of NVQs
- access to assessment
- assessment methods
- administration of assessor and verifier selection and training
- providing a recognised appeals procedure
- monitoring and evaluation arrangements.

By addressing such issues, awarding bodies are working to remove any remaining barriers that create access problems for both learners and providers. Detailed information is available from the awarding bodies themselves.

Removing barriers to achievement

1 Putting people first: the NVQ system has removed the traditional barriers to qualifications, shifting the emphasis from institutional requirements to individuals' achievement.

   (a) NVQs and the NVQ framework provide open access to assessment and clearly stated competence targets and progression routes;

(b) The National Database makes public and available to all information on qualifications, and assessment requirements. It provides users with the facility to map progression routes through the system;

(c) The National Record gives individuals control of their movement through the system, a means to record their experience and achievement, set targets and timeframes, and continuously assess progress.

2 No entry barriers: NVQs have no unnecessary entry requirements such as age, previous qualifications, specified length of experience – anyone can put themselves forward for assessment. NVQs necessitate that informed guidance, counselling and initial assessment replace arbitrary entry requirements.

3 Credit accumulation: NVQs unit credit design gives people greater choice in how they get qualified. Credits can be accumulated as and when the individual wishes. Career breaks no longer mean missing out on completing qualifications. Unit credits enable those re-entering training to gain early endorsement of their competence.

NVQ unit credits also allow those with learning difficulties, or disabilities, for some of whom a full NVQ may not be a realistic goal, to gain valuable credits within the qualifications system.

4 Flexible modes of learning: NVQs have no specified time/mode of learning or learning location. Because neither the time spent nor mode of learning are specified, NVQs offer greater flexibility in the way people can achieve qualifications. Individual circumstances, learning style preferences, employment priorities, special needs, can be taken into account, and programmes of learning tailor-made to suit individual requirements. It is this decoupling of learning from assessment that allows NVQs to meet individuals' learning needs in the context of a system built on national standards.

5 Access to assessment: the NVQ system has been designed to increase access to qualifications by enabling flexibility in assessment, so that individuals can gain credits towards a qualification as they so wish.

The range of assessment methods and contexts that

have developed within NVQs increase individual access to qualifications. NCVQ is working with awarding bodies to produce increasingly positive, flexible and responsive assessment strategies. The recognition of the significance of workplace assessment, and the emphasis in NVQs on performance evidence, has redressed the balance in a qualifications system skewed towards written knowledge testing. Written tests are appropriate only to certain types of assessment evidence and only to the level of the literacy standards demanded for the NVQ.

6 NVQs and the Accreditation of Prior Learning (APL): many awarding bodies are developing policies to enable recognition of evidence of achievement from candidates' previous work experience and other activities. These can be used as the basis for credits towards NVQ units. The evidence may be in the form of artefacts, e.g. photographs, documents, or evidence from third parties such as references/testimonials. Credits achieved act as an incentive to undertake further training to gain the full qualifications without undertaking unnecessary training and assessment in areas where the individual is already competent.

These developments will help to bring greater participation in vocational education and training, particularly from those whose work and previously unrecognised experience can now be credited in the national system. The National Record is available to help candidates present their previous experience and achievements in a common format.

7 Clear routes of progression: lack of coherence in the qualifications system and lack of information about the relation between one qualification and another, have in the past hampered individual achievement. Now, however, the NVQ framework, accessed through the National Database, shows how qualifications relate to each other. Information on qualifications and the various routes to their acquisition are available to all. This helps learners to take greater control in building on their past achievements and mapping their routes forward. The NVQ framework also helps the guidance and learning providers to match the individual's learning needs with the requirements of a national system.

8 The National Record of Achievement: The National Record plays an essential role in increasing access to qualifications and helps individuals make full use of the qualifications system. Through the action plan individuals determine qualifications targets and direct their career plan. Within the other sections of the National Record individuals have an accumulated portfolio of their achievements to present to employers at interview, and as a basis for negotiating further training and qualifications throughout a lifetime's learning.

Chapter 3

APL and the experience of different ethnic communities in Britain

In our introduction we saw that members of certain ethnic communities suffer from higher unemployment rates than others, and also that within certain groups a high proportion of people have no qualifications. In this chapter we are going to examine some of the reasons which could account for this and consider whether APL can be used as a means of improving opportunities. If we look at the educational experience of the Afro-Caribbean community, for example, it has often been stated that the British education system has failed to meet their needs and that young black people growing up in Britain often do not achieve their full potential. This is not surprising in a system which has traditionally failed to recognise and value the different cultural backgrounds and experiences of members of the black communities and which has remained inherently racist, in spite of 'multi-cultural' and 'anti-racist' policies developed and disseminated over the years. This is not to deny that there has been considerable effort and progress, particularly in certain areas, towards developing a more equal society with a more equitable education system. Nevertheless, racism remains endemic and does have an effect on the development and prospects of a substantial sector of society.

LANGUAGE, DIALECT AND RACISM

A major issue, which we will be looking at further in Chapter 5, is that of language. In this category we include languages such as those of the Indian sub-continent or African languages, Creole languages from the Caribbean and varieties of English spoken in this country by people with different language backgrounds. Two serious barriers affect speakers of other languages and

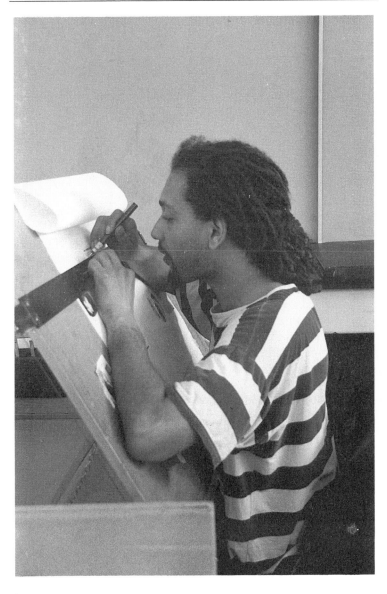

© Lenny Peters

varieties of English. One is that there is a universal failure to recognise the value of the ability to speak those other languages or varieties. The other is a persistent confusion between the ability to speak standard English and a person's general intelligence or ability. This has meant that, generally speaking, individuals are given no credit for being able to speak another, and often more than one other, language. On the contrary, they are often led to perceive this linguistic ability as a disadvantage. It has also meant that people from other language backgrounds have often had less value accorded to their other skills and abilities, with a corresponding lowering of their self-esteem and expectations of themselves. There is ample documented evidence of this in publications such as those produced by the Further Education Unit (FEU): *FE in Black and White* (1987) and *Language, Learning and Race* (1988). Margaret Robson says in the latter: 'the structures and practices both of educational institutions and wider society, to the extent that these are racist, affect the learning and potential of black students' (Robson 1988).

This can be illustrated by two quotes from staff in colleges interviewed for *FE in Black and White*, the first describing a vocational preparation course with an 84 per cent black intake: 'By having such a large ethnic minority intake the course will be devalued and that will serve to bring about its downfall' (FEU 1987).

The second quote concerns finding work placements for students: 'There are certain places where I am reluctant to send coloured students for their own sake' (FEU 1987). One of the findings of *FE in Black and White* is that black students tend to be located on some courses and not others, and that in particular they are not getting through to higher level vocational courses. Research has shown that black people recognise the importance of vocational qualifications as much as, if not more than, white people but sometimes feel that further education is not a route which can lead them to employment. This may be due to the fact that for many of them their past experience of education has been negative.

People from ethnic minority communities who came to Britain as adults have often worked for years in manual jobs before turning towards education or training, with a view to developing their potential or because of redundancy. In this context, again, language is often used as a pretext for not giving someone a job or promotion, or for making them redundant, where in times of expansion language would not have been an issue. An example of this is quoted in *Current Issues in Teaching English as a Second Language to Adults*:

> In 1977, seven Bangladeshi workers won a case against the British Steel Corporation when it refused to reinstate them in posts they had already satisfactorily held down and for which it was now claimed their literacy in English was inadequate. BSC was found guilty of violating the 1976 Race Relations Act on indirect discrimination and had to reinstate the workers.
>
> (Nicholls and Hoadley-Maidment (eds) 1988)

APL AND THE DIFFERENT ETHNIC COMMUNITIES

People from different ethnic communities who are seeking qualifications through education or training have a right to assessment and accreditation procedures which take into account and value their past experience. Writing about assessment and accreditation in *Current Issues in Teaching English as a Second Language to Adults*, Sheila Rosenberg says:

> One way of countering cultural hegemony is to make greater use of continuous assessment and profiling, devise appropriate tasks, and ensure well-briefed and sympathetic assessors. However it still remains the duty of national examining boards to recognise and not penalise cultural diversity, and to reward bilingualism positively.
>
> (Rosenberg in Nicholls and Hoadley-Maidment (eds) 1988)

This points the way to two main tasks for successful APL for candidates from different ethnic communities. One is to ensure that the competences and criteria drawn up for the recognition of any particular skill or ability should avoid ethnocentricity and recognise the experience of people from the different communities. The second is to ensure that appropriate awareness training is provided for counsellors, assessors and verifiers, as well as ensuring that counsellors, assessors and verifiers whose linguistic and cultural backgrounds reflect those of the candidates, are available. In this way means can be found of accrediting prior experience and learning which relate to the experience of being black, and which recognise the positive attributes of that experience.

One way in which diversity of experience can be recognised is in the qualification itself, so that skills such as Indian vegetarian cookery, Chinese cookery, Halal (Muslim ritual) butchery, Afro hairdressing, preparing costumes for the Notting Hill carnival, providing a make-up service for Hindu weddings and Asian dressmaking can be accepted as valid for recognised qualifications. This has been exemplified by the CGLI and the RSA, which have attempted to devise qualifications for particular vocational areas which may attract people from different ethnic groups. However, the initiative also rests with advisers and course tutors to adapt their programme to fit the clientele, at the same time as operating within the constraints of the system. This can constitute either a weakness or a strength of the concept of APL. If the advisers are aware and able they can render the process sensitive to a variety of situations, but if the process becomes standardised in a restrictive way, because of the manner in which it is implemented, it could become a negative experience for those whose skills lie in specialised areas. The process needs to be flexible enough to cope with different ways of achieving results as well as different products. An experienced and talented cook may not be familiar with British weights and measures, many highly skilled dressmakers never use a paper pattern, beauty and hair care for different types of skin and hair will involve very different products and techniques, and concepts of what is beautiful will differ according to culture.

Guidance

If we look back at the description of the process of APL in Chapter 2 we see that Prior Learning Achievement refers to the totality of what someone knows, understands and can do at the time of assessment. In order to claim an achievement candidates will need to demonstrate to the assessor the knowledge or skill they are claiming, and provide evidence to support it. The role of the adviser or counsellor, as they are variously known, will clearly be all the more crucial if:

1 Candidates have had negative past experiences and have low estimations of their achievements.
2 Candidates have come from different backgrounds and are unfamiliar with the system and society as a whole in this country.

We shall be looking at some of the difficulties faced by people with qualifications from overseas in the next chapter, but whether they are qualified or not, many people arriving in a new country to start a new life may feel reluctant to mull over the past, either because they wish to make a clean break and a new start, or because they do not feel that their past experience is valuable or relevant to their present aspirations. If they do not claim credit for past achievement at work it may be because they are unwilling or unable to contact employers in their country of origin, particularly if they are refugees. A counsellor wishing to guide through the APL process people who have come from developing countries will need to have an understanding of the vastly different life experiences, and correspondingly different skills that people will bring with them. First of all, they will probably have experienced very different teaching and learning methods in formal education, and will therefore need to gain an understanding of the system in Britain, and in particular the relationship between teacher and learner. Second, the skills and knowledge that they bring will have been acquired in a very different context. In a pre-technological society, for example, mathematical concepts such as the decimal place may not have been relevant because more general concepts were used, such as 'a large number of cattle', and the experiences of day-to-day living, caring, cooking, working, in a rural developing country will have had little in common with a capitalist, free-market, permissive society such as this. For example, a young woman student in an FE college, with a good secondary education record from her country, described how she spent the school holidays back home in Uganda:

> I went to my grandmother's village. There we used to get up early to fetch water and wood to cook breakfast. All day we worked in the fields, growing cassava. The cassava is peeled and chopped and ground to be made into flour to make our bread. In the evenings we cooked again on the wood fires, then we sat around the fire every evening singing and telling stories.

This young woman was mature, well organised and conscientious. She had been working and taking responsibility for others and for organisational matters from an early age. She had always been used to operating as one of a team and taking into consideration the needs of others around her. She had learnt to be practical and economical as a necessity. She applied and was accepted on a nursing course in this country, for which she seemed eminently suited.

The APL adviser/counsellor working with people from different ethnic backgrounds thus faces the delicate tasks of:

1 familiarising candidates with a process which may seem strange and inappropriate to them initially;
2 understanding the context of the candidates' experience and extrapolating from it their acquired skills and knowledge;
3 assessing the transfer value of those skills or knowledge to other situations.

Obviously an adviser/counsellor with a similar background to the candidate may be at an advantage if they have the appropriate counselling skills but it is not realistic to suppose that this could always, or often, be the case. Training in cross-cultural counselling is a more realistic goal and one which institutions implementing APL would be well advised to adopt if they are not already doing so. A check list of: 'some tentative guidelines for those involved in Cross-Cultural Counselling' was published in *Multiracial Education*, the journal of the National Association for Multiracial Education, as long ago as 1983 and includes a number of points which seem applicable in the context of APL (Lago and Ball 1983). The following list has been adapted from theirs:

1 To be able to provide a warm, caring, non-judgmental atmosphere within which the client can feel safe to trust.
2 To have a genuine interest in and knowledge of the client's culture.
3 To develop awareness of one's own cultural framework and how this may differ from that of the client.
4 To be aware of one's own cultural norms about verbal and non-verbal communication.
5 To consider carefully many ethical concepts, including confidentiality, their role in the situation, their underlying philosophy, all of which may have very different connotations for the client.
6 To establish a clear contract based on a mutual understanding of assumptions and expectations.

7 To be aware that notions of autonomy and self-determination may well be different in other cultures.
8 To suspend initial assumptions and hold back immediate reactions to situations.
9 To receive training, supervision and support, the training to include the various dimensions of race awareness and an understanding of the manifestations of racism.

Assessment

When a counsellor has successfully helped a candidate to identify, gather and compile evidence it will be the role of the assessor to judge the quality of the evidence and attach a credit level and value to it. The assessor will be interviewing candidates and discussing the evidence with them so it will obviously be essential to apply the same training requirements as for counsellors, in terms of race awareness and cross-cultural understanding. It would be disastrous for the morale of APL candidates to build up a relationship of trust and understanding with a counsellor and produce a portfolio of evidence, only to have it rejected by an assessor through a lack of understanding. In an article in *Adults Learning* we quoted the example of a person being assessed for CGLI 201 getting into difficulties because his previous training had taken place in Canada and he was wiring circuits to North American standards (McKelvey and Peters 1991). Fortunately he had the language skills to make the assessor aware of the problem, which was then taken into account in his assessment.

The importance of the APL process in terms of opening up avenues to vocational qualifications and higher education to a sector of the population which has historically been under-represented in those areas would be tragically undermined if the conditions which create equality of opportunity in the system are not applied throughout the process, from initial counselling through to verification and certification by an awarding body. A project carried out by the Unit for the Development of Adult and Continuing Education (UDACE) between 1989 and 1992, identi-fied the issues of level and credit, among others, as requiring further attention. It says: 'As the boundaries between higher education and other forms of education and training become more permeable, it is important to understand how level is being defined across sectoral boundaries and seek a consensus on this.'

Further, 'Work is needed on the notion of credit, and how it can be defined to ease transition between higher, further, adult and work based learning' *(Learning Outcomes in Higher Education* 1992).

The unit stressed the importance of developing appropriate methods of assessment in higher education which correspond to those used outside, and thus ensuring continuity and progress for students. These issues are of particular relevance to people from different ethnic backgrounds who have suffered in the past through the inflexibility of institutions and the failure of the education system to cater for their needs.

Higher education and people from different ethnic groups

Alongside women and working-class students, black people and those from other ethnic groups are currently under-represented in higher education, in spite of the development of access courses, and other attempts to broaden the range of student intake. Many institutions still perceive these initiatives as a threat to tradition and to standards of excellence. In her report on the *Access and Staff Development Project* (1992) conducted at Birkbeck College, University of London, a college which caters exclusively for mature, part-time students, Margaret Andrews points out that during the 1991–2 Academic Year nearly 60 per cent of the student intake had standard university qualifications. So in one of Britain's most multiracial cities, an institution seemingly designed to cater for a non-traditional student intake is nonetheless choosing to recruit a majority of students who have followed traditional routes. The project, which was initiated with the aim of widening access to Birkbeck College, included the following amongst its recommendations:

- guidelines for admissions tutors to help them assess mature students' prior experience and learning
- staff training to raise awareness of non-standard qualifications among admissions staff
- the setting of targets for recruiting non-traditional entrants.

As far as the views of applicants to the college were concerned, the project found that 'They were anxious that their life skills would be perceived as inappropriate for a part-time degree at Birkbeck' (Andrews 1992).

Andrews reports that studies have shown such perceptions to be consistent with those of mature applicants to other higher education institutions, and cites in particular a 1992 project at Bristol Polytechnic to widen access to higher education for black people. Another finding, resulting from a survey of undergraduates at Birkbeck, showed that only about a third of those questioned were aware that previous educational experience could reduce the number of years they would have to study for their degree. So existing research tends to demonstrate, on the one hand, a lack of familiarity with APL procedures in higher education institutions and, on the other, a lack of confidence among potential students concerning the value of their past experience.

Cultural assumptions about what is valuable

Ultimately, this is the key issue in considering APL with people of different ethnic backgrounds and particularly when working with those who suffer double or triple discrimination, such as women, people with disabilities and working-class people who are black or from other ethnic groups. To refer back again to some of the statistics given in the introduction, we quoted 52 per cent of men and 68 per cent of women from Pakistan and Bangladesh as having no qualification, which is approximately double the figure for the rest of the population. This high percentage is no doubt partly due to the high proportion of manual workers in those communities, but the figure for women is certainly related to cultural notions of the appropriacy of education for women and their role in the home and in society. To quote Amrit Wilson in *Finding a Voice: Asian Women in Britain*:

> It is often said that Muslim men think it a matter of pride that their women shouldn't work . . . 'Work' in this statement does not include housework, ill-paid home sewing or the heavy work of carrying food to the fields in Pakistan. What Muslim men don't like is for their women to work outside the home, potentially in the company of strange men. These attitudes are created by *Izzat*, the sensitive and many faceted male family identity which can change as the situation demands it – from family pride to honour to self respect, and sometimes to pure male ego.
>
> (Wilson 1978)

She goes on to outline the situation for women in Britain: 'In Britain *Izzat* faces a whole new range of threats. Should girls brought up in Britain be allowed to go on to further education? Should they be allowed to take jobs? Can their marriages be delayed?' (Wilson 1978).

This situation is, of course, evolving, in that among the younger generation more women are going on to further and higher education, but they are still a very small minority. Another publication, *Breaking the Silence* gives some insight into the conflict experienced by Asian women from different communities struggling to survive and progress in a hostile environment. The editor, Manjula Mukherjee, writes in her introduction: 'I can realise there is a great urge among the second and third generation of young women to rebel against the tradition up to a certain extent' (Mukherjee (ed.) 1984).

A young Indian woman writes about not being allowed to go to college and not being brave enough to put pressure on her parents. Others say: 'Courage is what it really boils down to, whether or not a woman has the courage to live the way she wants to' (ibid.). Or, from a woman who got divorced and succeeded in becoming an SRN: 'Remember girls that you are not alone and you need not suffer if you have the courage and strength and tremendous will power, that is the key to success' (ibid.).

But a woman from Bangladesh, married and with a daughter, says:

> It is shame and funny still today we value British degree. Many of my friends who could not or can't gain British degree, they feel great deal of shame and failure inside them. It does not matter how much money or how expensive house or car we got – we have got great weakness and respect for British education.
>
> (ibid.)

With the high motivation and tremendous determination that they bring to education it seems the least that education could offer them would be a recognition of where they are coming from and of the struggles they have had and will have to contend with to achieve their ambitions. APL could be the first step along the road for a great number of women, young and old who have run homes and extended families, done paid work in the home such as machining or packing, or worked in family businesses, and been involved in the life of their community. A good example of this is two Asian sisters on a Return to Learn course, who were interviewed as part of a survey to discover the extent of their transferable skills at the start of the course. The older sister, aged 25, was assisting her husband to run a travel agency catering for the community, and was doing all the secretarial and clerical work involved. On Saturdays, she and her sister, aged 22, regularly cooked for 200 people attending the local mosque. These women were eligible for accreditation for clerical and secretarial units of qualifications as well as catering units, but needed appropriate guidance from someone with an understanding of the community situation. They were also held back by being classified as ESOL (English for Speakers of Other Languages) students. The structure of some FE colleges is such that ESOL provision is segregated from vocational departments and routes to qualifications, and students spend long periods of time 'improving their English' while their other skills are overlooked.

People with disabilities or learning difficulties from black and ethnic minority communities

Issues around APL and people with disabilities or learning difficulties are dealt with in a subsequent chapter, but it is worth mentioning here that attitudes to and expectations of people with disabilities or learning difficulties vary in different cultures. In developing economies where welfare benefits do not exist and day centres and training programmes are few and far between, people with disabilities are often made to feel that they are a burden on their families and on society. At the same time they may have had to lead very sheltered and isolated lives with extremely low expectations of what they could achieve. An Indian woman aged 40, a wheelchair user owing to a condition she had from birth, had missed out completely on education as a child. Although she had her own flat and did her own shopping and cooking, her daytime activities were limited to attending a local day centre where educational provision had been cut and the supply of piece work from local firms had dried up. With support and guidance she was able to draw up a plan to continue her education at a voluntary centre which was easily accessible, and develop her computing skills with a view to working from home or possibly obtaining employment in the future.

Although similar cases may arise equally with disabled people born in Britain, it is nevertheless crucial that cultural distinctions are taken into account when counselling people with disabilities for APL purposes, just as it is for those who are able-bodied. The following exercise can be used as an introduction to the APL process, and at the same time serve to raise awareness of cultural differences and the variety of experience that candidates may present.

EXERCISE

Participants form groups of three and take the roles of observer, interviewer and candidate.

The candidate is given a role sheet specifying a person's background, experience and qualifications. Role sheets should be prepared to give examples of the range of candidates likely to present themselves, in terms of ethnicity, age and past experience.

The interviewer is asked to gain information on the candidate's:

- personal characteristics
- special needs
- interests
- attitudes towards learning
- abilities and strengths
- training needs
- evidence which could be used to substantiate claims.

The exercise should be designed so that some candidates have skills/direction/knowledge that can have competence assessed straightaway, some are without clear direction, and some have knowledge/skills in a number of different areas. Two brief sample role sheets are included here, followed by an example of a form filled in by a genuine APL candidate detailing her past experience, and including some of the information the exercise is designed to elicit.

Role sheets

Mohammad Mussa Omar is 25 years old. He left Eritrea two years ago and came as a refugee to live in London. He worked as a motor mechanic in Eritrea, repairing cars and military vehicles. He finished his education in Eritrea at the age of 16. He speaks

Tigrina, Amharic and English. Since arriving in England he has taken several ESOL courses and his spoken language is good. To support his wife and child he repairs cars on a casual basis and has recently found a Saturday job in a local garage. He would like to obtain a qualification in motor mechanics and get a full-time job.

Najma Hussain is a 29-year-old mother of two. She was born in Pakistan but came to the UK at the age of nine and has attended special schools, as well as a mainstream secondary school, due to having partial hearing from birth. She left school with no qualifications but can communicate well in English through lip reading and sign language. Her husband runs his own business and she has always helped him with ordering stock, staff rotas, banking and accounting. She is also heavily involved with a self-help voluntary community group aimed at improving the social life of people who are deaf or have partial hearing. She has been treasurer of the group and is an active fundraiser and campaigner. She would like to gain a qualification either in business administration or in the area of social work.

ACCREDITATION OF PRIOR LEARNING
STAGE 1 – PAST EXPERIENCE
LIST WHAT YOU HAVE DONE IN THE PAST UNDER THE
FOLLOWING HEADINGS

EDUCATION/TRAINING

INFANTS SCHOOL
PRIMARY SCHOOL
SECONDARY SCHOOL
6th FORM COLLEGE
COLLEGE - EVENING - ENGLISH LANG

EMPLOYMENT

I WORKED AS A JUNIOR SECRETARY FOR FIRM OF ACCOUNTANTS IN 1982.
I then worked for another firm of Accountants as a schedule typist/WP operator, working for two in the tax department and processing schedules for another five. Also some reception, telex, fax and photocopying work.
                                                    P.T.O.

VOLUNTARY WORK

I have often participated in the Notting Hill Carnival, and have therefore helped to make the costumes.
I sometimes help out at local youth centre, helping the youth worker to organising trips to seaside, adventure playgrounds etc.

LIFE EXPERIENCES

I have enjoyed arranging and going on holidays especially St. Lucia.
I also enjoy organising leaving parties at work e.g. arranging collection and buying cards and presents and sending out invites.
I past my driving test — after two attempts!

I also had an evening job at Tesco, in order to earn some extra cash for Christmas.

Employment continued from previous page

I was promoted in 1988 to Admin Assistant/Group Manager's secretary. My duties included typing, for Group Manager and taking and receiving making calls to clients and other staff.
I also had admin. duties for my group (30). The group mainly consisted of students who were going through their three year study for Chartered Accountants exam. I had to deal with all new students, showing them around the office and making sure they had all necessary papers, documents etc. I also looked after them during their employment, checking that they had the correct dates for their courses and also planning their job structures e.g. sending them out on audit jobs. I also kept a record of sickness and holiday records for the whole of the group. I posted timesheets and bills of IBM computers. Opened and distributed letters and memos, kept groups correspondence files up to date. Updated database.

I now work as a temporary secretary at The —— Hospital. My duties include Receptionist to all visitors, Answering all calls, typing letters, reports, specifications, meeting minutes, contract admin. forms. Maintaining and ordering stationery. Plan and drawing printing. Sending questionnaires and letters to contractors and maintaining contractor's list on computer.

ACCREDITATION OF PRIOR LEARNING
STAGE 2 – PAST EXPERIENCE
CONSIDER WHAT SORT OF THINGS YOU LEARNED IN EACH
EXPERIENCE

EDUCATION/TRAINING

My Qualifications include English Lang. & R.E.
O'Level.
City & Guilds Community Studies. CSE Maths,
History, French, Community Studies, Biology

EMPLOYMENT

I have learned a lot from my employment, and
have met and made a lot of friends. I have
had the opportunity to train on wps, computers,
telexs, fax, photocopiers etc.

VOLUNTARY WORK

I achieved a great team spirit whilst working
with other people preparing costumes for the
Carnival.

LIFE EXPERIENCES

ACCREDITATION OF PRIOR LEARNING
STAGE 3 – PAST EXPERIENCE
WHAT WERE THE OUTCOMES OF THE LEARNING? SPECIFY
THIS IN TERMS OF SKILLS/KNOWLEDGE/SUCCESS/FAILURE

EDUCATION/TRAINING

My City & Guilds Community Studies Course
incorporated a day morning at a physically
handicapped school & a morning at a playschool.
I enjoyed this because I found that I liked
being with these children and helping them with their studies.

EMPLOYMENT

VOLUNTARY WORK

LIFE EXPERIENCES

ACCREDITATION OF PRIOR LEARNING
STAGE 4 – FUTURE PLANS

USE THE LEARNING OUTCOMES YOU IDENTIFIED IN STAGE 3 TO DRAW UP A LIST OF YOUR STRENGTHS (ie. skills/knowledge you possess)

STRENGTHS:

I have good computer knowledge.
I get on well with people, especially people I work with.
I am quite conscientious and take a pride in my work.
I have a sense of humour.
Good at written communication.

NOW USE THE LEARNING OUTCOMES YOU IDENTIFIED IN STAGE 3 TO DRAW UP A LIST OF YOUR DEVELOPMENT NEEDS (ie. skills/knowledge you want to acquire)

I am lacking in confidence.
I also need improvement with my verbal communication.
Processing petty cash and invoices & also payroll.
I would like to learn more about Business Studies.
I would also like to learn more about organisation – supervising.

ACCREDITATION OF PRIOR LEARNING
STAGE 5 – FUTURE PLANS
CONSIDER THE DEVELOPMENT NEEDS YOU HAVE IDENTIFIED,
AND DECIDE WHICH THINGS ARE A PRIORITY AND WHY.

WHAT? | WHY?

Confidence & Communication — I feel that my lack of communication often lets my down, especially in interviews. I know I have the ability to do things but I do not always have the confidence. This is something I would like to improve.

Administration, petty cash, invoices & payroll — In my previous job I was involved in a lot of administration work, but I find that I now do mostly typing and telephone work, I would therefore like to brush up on these skills.

Business studies — I would very much like to continue studying. Maybe the Bus. Admin. Level III or the BTEC Business Studies Course.

ACCREDITATION OF PRIOR LEARNING
STAGE 6 – ACTION PLANNING
KNOWLEDGE/SKILL TO BE DEVELOPED:

AIMS: (why?)

OUTCOMES: (what will you be able to do afterwards?)

METHOD: (pattern of learning/content/tasks)

CRITERIA FOR ACHIEVEMENT: (specific/measurable)

HOW WILL THIS BE EVIDENCED/DEMONSTRATED?

COMPLETION DATE SET:

ACHIEVED:

Chapter 4

Recognition of qualifications and experience from overseas

Large numbers of black adults in Britain have overseas qualifications. Many of them also have experience, sometimes very substantial, in their field of work, either in their country of origin or in other countries around the world. However, there is an enormous waste of skills and ability taking place because of the lack of adequate procedures for the recognition and accreditation of qualifications and experience. Many of the issues which were raised in the previous chapter: language, cultural values, matching of levels and credit, and negative past experience in this country, including racism, arise with a vengeance when it comes to attempting to obtain recognition, particularly for qualifications and experience gained outside Europe. In the case of refugees and other new arrivals these issues are complicated by questions of residency status and entitlement to work, and grants for further study, which create acute financial difficulties for the people concerned.

The result is not only the waste of a valuable source of professional expertise and person power, but also the creation of a substantial body of people who experience feelings of disillusion, frustration, disappointment and often anger at the situation in which they find themselves. APL has obvious potential as a means of overcoming some of the barriers facing overseas qualified people, but there is still a long way to go towards the setting up of a comprehensive system, accessible to all, which functions efficiently and economically.

In particular, work is needed to ensure that individuals with overseas qualifications are fully aware of the options open to them, through the building up of more efficient publicity networks in the community. APL advisers face a difficult and

time-consuming task as, in addition to the role of fact-finding and negotiating outcomes for and with the candidate, they will need considerable tact and understanding. The process has the potential to cause distress to participants forced to confront the harsh facts of discrimination and prejudice in British society, at the same time as coping with the trauma of having been uprooted and displaced from their home to start a new life.

Guidance, information and support for individuals are essential – advisers must be trained not only to understand fully the APL process and its applications, but also to be able to guide candidates through the technical language of competence and assessment. Recruiting assessors from a range of linguistic and cultural backgrounds should lower the risk of bias or racist practices, but training for assessors and monitoring the progress of individuals through the APL process is none the less important.

Finding a job, even with a recognised British qualification, can be a lengthy and difficult process, but guidance workers can help by making sure that they are aware of employment trends, any local or regional trends developments, and by being able to put clients in touch with agencies or professional groups which may be able to offer more information or assistance. The World University Service (WUS) provides specific information on the recognition of experience and qualifications of doctors and lawyers from overseas. There are some particular difficulties for candidates in these professions; the WUS, for example, has raised the issue of racism in the legal profession in the UK, citing the criteria for acceptability into chambers for solicitors or barristers, which are, apparently, compatibility, turnout and demeanour, and the ability to speak articulately. These areas are explored in more detail on pp. 67–73.

EQUIVALENCING QUALIFICATIONS

In the absence of an official Qualification Recognition Service in Britain, the National Academic Recognition Information Centre (NARIC) of the British Council, until 1991, provided a service for individuals whereby they could write in with copies and translations of their certificates in order to be informed of how their qualifications related to British qualifications. However, NARIC made it clear to applicants that:

there is no official equivalence of overseas and British qualifications in Britain. British educational and professional institutions are autonomous and as such reserve the right to make
their own decisions on the acceptability and recognition to be
accorded to any overseas qualification . . .

(NARIC 1992)

Current procedure is, if anything, less accessible to the individual.
The services of NARIC are now only available to institutions and
employers or through the careers service or job centres. Individuals wishing to gain information on the equivalence of their
qualifications have to approach an institution or service and ask
them to contact NARIC on their behalf. The alternative is for
institutions to purchase a copy of *The International Guide to
Qualifications in Education*, produced by the National Academic
Recognition Information Centre (1991) at a cost of £90, and
provide their own guidance service to advise candidates. The
system is clearly not designed for easy access to information
about equivalences and the fact that individuals cannot approach
NARIC direct has obvious implications for both accessibility and
cost in terms of the time of staff involved in advising candidates,
and consulting NARIC on their behalf.

When they do gain access to the information, individuals and
guidance workers will find that there is considerable variation in
what information is offered in relation to qualifications from
different countries. For example, for Greece or Sri Lanka the
equivalence of specific grades obtained in examinations corresponding to GCSE and 'A' level is given, whereas for Somalia no
information is available on the grading of secondary level
qualifications, with the result that Somalis who have completed
secondary education still have to complete a year on an access
course before being accepted on degree courses. For degrees
obtained in India the detail is such that not only where the degree
was obtained is relevant but also when. A candidate for equivalence with a First Class Honours Degree in Economics from Delhi
University, for example, was told that because she had been
awarded her degree in 1971 it would not be considered
equivalent to a British degree, because the standard that year was
not suitable, although in previous and subsequent years it was.
Equivalences are clearly established on the basis of statistical
evidence rather than on course content, and it is understandable

that considerable frustration is experienced by those who have worked long and hard to achieve professional status when their achievement is devalued in their new country of residence.

Further difficulties arise when qualifications are recognised as valuable towards a British qualification but not equivalent to a whole qualification. Although this would seem to be better than nothing it can often give rise to more frustration, because Credit Accumulation and Transfer Schemes (CATS) are not yet in operation in many institutions, and where they are it will still be necessary to identify units of credit in the candidate's past experience which correspond to units in the scheme, so that appropriate reductions in the time of further study can be allowed (see Chapter 2). The identification of equivalence, and negotiation with institutions on credit value, are appropriate tasks for an APL guidance worker and difficult for candidates, especially if new to this country, to achieve on their own. However, they can be extremely time consuming, which has a bearing on the cost of the process. A good example of this kind of work is the Accreditation and Recognition of Refugee Professional Qualification Support and Guidance Project running at Bournville College of FE in Birmingham. The project provides individual assessment, guidance and support for groups of ten refugees, over a period of ten to twelve weeks, including a work placement where appropriate for the purpose of practical assessment, with the aim of achieving:

- UK recognition of the qualifications held by the participants.
- An understanding, for the participants, of the professional environment in Britain relating to their specialism.
- An assessment of the specialist English language needs of the participants.

The inclusion of work experience was a response to the obvious difficulty of providing evidence of work experience for refugees, who may have left their country with very few belongings and documents and may not be in a position to make contact with former employers. The project has also highlighted the length of the recognition procedure and the amount of work involved for the guidance worker in negotiating with professional bodies, sometimes fruitlessly. However, some of the positive outcomes have been the exemption from Level 1 of the ACCA course at Birmingham Polytechnic for a candidate already qualified as an accountant in his country, and the according of two years' credit towards the City and Guilds 730, Certificate of Education, for participants who had teaching experience in their country of origin. This credit was obtained in one case through the construction of a portfolio including lesson plans and materials from work experience, and in the other through accreditation of the candidate's qualification in his country of origin.

It is interesting to note, however, that the latter candidate had gained two qualifications at recognised higher education institutions in Britain, one a B.Phil. in Education in 1990 and the other a Diploma in the Teaching of English for Specific Purposes in 1991, before coming to Britain as a refugee in 1992, yet these qualifications were not recognised for the purpose of teaching English in the UK. This is not the only instance of qualifications gained in Britain by students from other countries being discounted when the person subsequently settles here. NIACE quote the example of a Ugandan Doctor of Medicine with an MSc in Clinical Tropical Medicine from the University of London, and a Diploma in Tropical Medicine and Hygiene from the Royal College of Physicians, who was told he would have to go back to medical school in order to practise in this country because his medical degree in Uganda was accepted by the General Medical Council 'for the purposes of limited registration only'.

Some of the general conclusions from the first group to go through the process at Bournville, were:

- the need for plenty of time for the adviser/guidance worker to network and negotiate with institutions and professional bodies
- the need for group work, to foster mutual support and for the participants to learn from each other's experiences
- the need for English language support during the process of accreditation as well as intensive language training for some of the participants.

Language issues around accreditation of overseas qualifications

Obviously, when people with qualifications, whatever the level, arrive in Britain with no, or very little, knowledge of the English language, the logical first step will probably be intensive language tuition. Even at the earliest stages of learning the language, however, advice and guidance are essential, from someone who is familiar with the range of possible classes available and preferably from someone who speaks a language familiar to the new arrival. For a qualified person, it will make a huge difference whether they start in a once weekly adult education class, alongside students who may have had very little previous education, or on an intensive course geared towards people with successful educational experience behind them. The key issue, however, is the progression routes available, and it is often after the initial stages, when a certain level of language has been attained, that things will start to get difficult.

There are plenty of examples of young people with 'A'level equivalent qualifications being referred to the Business and Technology Education Council (BTEC) first level courses, for example, and there may be circumstances where this is the most appropriate course, but often it is simply because they are young and the course is there. Another example is the new arrival who says 'I want to go to university', and is referred to an access course, despite having the necessary qualifications for entry to university, or having already started a course in higher education in another country. Again, this may be the most appropriate route in the absence of any preparatory course for higher education for speakers of other languages. This is where the role of the APL adviser will prove crucial in saving precious time and money by finding out the value of the student's qualifications and the credit that can be accorded. The lack of English language, as mentioned in the previous chapter, must not be allowed to detract from the value of the qualifications and experience a person has acquired. It can often be the case that a supposed lack of English language, which is actually an unfamiliarity or prejudice about an accent, on the part of the hearer, will be used as an excuse to turn down a candidate for study or employment. The APL adviser may need to act as an advocate for the candidate in these circumstances. There is certainly a need for awareness training for staff in educational institutions and for employers, as well as a need to offer support to candidates in preparing for interviews, self-presentation and confidence building. The issues around language for overseas qualified people thus include:

- The provision of intensive language courses for new arrivals.
- The provision of language for specific purposes, so that qualified people can learn the language of their specialism.

- The provision of training in interview techniques and self-advocacy.
- The training of advisers, advocates and assessors who understand the issues around language and either speak languages in common with candidates or can use interpreters.
- The provision of language awareness training for staff in educational institutions, employers and members of professional bodies.

Some examples of courses designed to cater for people with qualifications from overseas are:

- A project funded by British Petroleum and piloted at the City of London Polytechnic: Language Support for Higher Education Access Programme in East London (LSHAPE).
- A short course for Overseas Qualified People (OQP) at Newham Community College which has run in the summer term for the last five years.

LSHAPE

The LSHAPE course was conceived to cater for young people with the necessary qualifications for entry to higher education, but needing intensive English language and study skills but, in fact, on both the fifteen-week pilot and the subsequent one-year course the major response came from people in their twenties and thirties, some of whom had either completed a first degree or spent some time in higher education in their own country or another country.

Objectives of participants were:

- to enter higher education or complete the higher education they had started elsewhere
- to make a change of direction and pursue a different course from their first choice
- to undertake postgraduate study
- to obtain employment.

An essential element of the course is intensive counselling, which takes place on a weekly basis and is available in Bengali (the language of over 50 per cent of participants) and Somali. The other elements of the course are:

- English language (two sessions per week)
- study skills (one session per week)
- portfolio preparation and CV writing (one session per week)
- information technology (one session per week).

As well as the help they receive in having the value of their qualifications assessed and in choosing their way forward, participants improve their English language skills through extensive writing and work on oral presentations and interview skills. The information technology sessions enable them to produce CVs and project work to include in their portfolios, and they are able to familiarise themselves with methods of study in the UK through the study skills component.

Of the thirteen participants completing the one-year course:

- two were accepted for postgraduate study
- four were accepted for first degrees
- two went on to access courses because they felt they needed more preparation before entering higher education
- one was accepted on to the borough instructors' team as a trainee teacher
- one who is qualified as a doctor is preparing the Professional and Linguistic Assessment Board (PLAB) test
- one who is qualified as an accountant is experiencing difficulties joining an accountancy body
- two are unable to continue studying because of ineligibility for grants and are therefore seeking employment.

These outcomes raise a number of issues which need further discussion, including the financial difficulties experienced by new arrivals, and also some professional areas where particular problems arise, such as medicine, teaching, accountancy and law. However for the majority of the participants the outcomes were most satisfactory and all participants stressed the importance of the group as a resource for learning, support and confidence building.

OQP

The OQP course has, over the years, tended to cater for a slightly older age group although covering a wide age range. As it is a short course (ten weeks) it aims more at people whose English language is already of a fairly high standard. The aim of the course is to help professionally qualified people to orientate themselves within the British system and obtain jobs or training. It includes:

- information on relevant career opportunities in Britain, particularly in education, social services, local authorities, or the Health Service
- individual counselling and guidance
- portfolio preparation and CV writing
- interview skills
- assertiveness training.

The course has traditionally recruited a high proportion of qualified teachers who wish to carry on working in their chosen profession in Britain. Although their position has been helped by schemes such as the licensed teachers' and instructors' schemes, which enable them to start work and retrain, as well as a local scheme to recruit bilingual teachers into primary education, many of them still have to face the harsh fact that their qualifications are not considered equivalent, and they will be going into the job at a lower level than that at which they were working overseas. Many participants on OQP courses in Newham have found employment but in lower level work than their qualifications led them to expect, such as laboratory technician or nursery assistant for teachers, or clerical work for people with degrees in Economics or B.Comms. However, some have obtained full-time jobs in further or adult education and others have gained entry to higher education courses to update their skills.

The general feeling about this course has always been that it is too short. Participants have said that they need more time to improve their language skills and build their confidence, and more individual counselling with guidance on qualifications and equivalences.

This example again highlights the issue of teaching, and financial problems, as well as the recurring themes of sapped confidence, anger and frustration understandably experienced by people who are not able to fulfil their potential. The experience of the Birmingham project described above, and the LSHAPE and OQP examples, point to the group as an important source of mutual support and learning for candidates with qualifications from overseas going through the APL process.

Financial issues

The courses outlined above were offered free of charge to participants, in the case of LSHAPE because of external funding from BP. However, if in the future colleges wish to recoup costs for offering APL services the implications for people with overseas qualifications could be serious. Refugees and asylum seekers are not eligible to work during the first six months of their residency. When they do become eligible they may face difficulties finding employment because of lack of English language and if they do find work it will often be in low paid jobs with long hours, making attendance at college difficult. If, after undergoing the APL process, they find that further study is necessary to complete or update their qualifications, they will not be eligible for a grant until they have been resident in Britain for three years. Many of the people mentioned above opted for part-time courses as a solution to this problem, but where part-time courses were not on offer in the required specialism some were obliged to seek employment while waiting to become eligible for a grant. Understandably, the outcome of the APL process can lead to disappointment and frustration if clear routes are apparent but cannot be followed for financial reasons. This leads to three conclusions:

1 APL with guidance and advice should be offered free to unemployed people, particularly refugees and asylum seekers.
2 The facility should be offered in flexible modes to suit different needs.
3 Financial advice should be offered as part of the process.

Issues around teaching

In spite of periodical shortages of teachers in Britain, particularly in certain curriculum areas such as maths and science, and recently in the primary sector, teachers who trained outside Europe have consistently experienced difficulties in having their qualifications and experience recognised. They have faced the added insult of witnessing the importation of primary teachers from Holland, for example, while those already resident here, often with valuable bilingual skills, are rejected. The *Observer* quoted an example in 1988 of a young woman, born in Britain and having completed a three-year teacher training course in Jamaica and a BA at the University of the West Indies, who was offered a job at a London comprehensive school. In spite of being described by the headteacher as 'a highly articulate and conscientious teacher . . . who has a proven track record' she was refused a DES number, because her teacher training course in Jamaica was not considered comparable with the three-year course of teacher training in England and Wales (*Observer* 8 May 1988).

An advertisement for a course for overseas qualified teachers in the London Borough of Newham at around the same time drew no fewer than 100 responses, including a language teacher with a degree and teacher training from Colombia who was working as a minicab driver, and a woman with teacher training from India who wanted to become a nursery teacher and was working as a supervisor in a laundry. As previously stated, instructors' and licensed teachers' schemes offer hope and opportunities to people such as these but it is nevertheless depressing and demeaning for someone with training and several years of successful teaching behind them to re-enter the profession with the status of a trainee. For APL advisers working with teachers from overseas the task is therefore a delicate and difficult one and requires detailed knowledge of the different requirements and schemes in operation, which vary from one local authority to another and will no doubt become more complicated in the future. Advisers should also be aware that in the teaching profession undue emphasis may be placed on a candidate's English language skills as a factor related to their ability to control or communicate with a class. Whilst there is no question that communication skills are crucial for a successful teacher, teachers from overseas may need to gain confidence to assert that speaking with a particular accent or having learned English as a second language does not detract from their skills as teachers or from their expertise in their field.

EXERCISE

With the aim of helping course tutors to see that those with experiential learning often have knowledge and skills which exceed the minimum entry criteria for courses, the exercise takes place in three stages:

1 Course tutors are asked, together with others in their team, to look at the entry criteria for their course and rewrite them in terms of key competences required.

2 Participants are asked to think about what they would consider valid evidence of such competences.
3 Tutors are given sample or real portfolios from students and
   asked to evaluate them in terms of the entry criteria. The
   portfolios can be chosen to draw attention to different issues,
   e.g. people with overseas qualifications in engineering
   wanting to gain qualifications and get practical experience in
   Britain, or speakers of other languages wanting to study for the
   National Nursery Examination Board (NNEB).

An example of entry criteria in the form of competences devised
by tutors on an NNEB course was:

(a) Demonstrate a genuine interest in children – evidence of
    working with young children.
(b) Demonstrate ability to carry out verbal and written instructions.
(c) Demonstrate ability to write clearly – evidence of report/
    essay writing.

RECOGNITION OF OVERSEAS QUALIFICATIONS: DOCTORS

The World University Service (WUS) has issued an information
sheet on the Recognition of Overseas Qualifications for Doctors (the
text of which is set out below) in which they state that the standard
route to limited registration (for a maximum of five years) in the UK
for overseas doctors is the test conducted by the Professional and
Linguistic Assessment Board (PLAB). Doctors qualified in Australia,
Hong Kong, Malaysia, New Zealand, Singapore, the West Indies,
EEC countries and the Republic of Ireland are accepted for full registration. The PLAB test is expensive, stringent, and has a low pass
rate. There are courses which prepare candidates for the test and
which definitely give them a better chance of getting through, but in
most cases these will have to be paid for. Doctors who have not
completed an internship of at least twelve months, overseas, which
is recognised as satisfactory by the General Medical Council, cannot
apply for registration but will have to start a medical degree from
scratch, except in exceptional circumstances. Obviously this would
be a financial impossibility for most refugees, as well as a
disheartening process, and an adviser might do well to offer information about other related career prospects and courses where they
might be able to gain some credit for past achievement.

Background

In the UK doctors must be registered with the General Medical Council. There are two forms of registration for overseas qualified doctors: limited and full. Full registration allows doctors to undertake any kind of professional employment. Those overseas qualifications which are recognised for full registration by the GMC includes qualifications from Australia, Hong Kong, Malaysia, New Zealand, Singapore, West Indies, EEC countries and the Republic of Ireland. Most overseas qualifications, however, are accepted only for limited registration and for a maximum period of five years. Limited registration is only granted for employment which is supervised by a fully registered medical practitioner or for posts which have been approved for education and training purposes. Finally, there are overseas doctors who are not eligible for any kind of registration in the British Isles. In 1989, there were 5,546 overseas doctors with limited registration and 2,183 with full registration.

This report will deal only with limited registration and those qualifications not admitted for any kind of registration.

Limited registration

Doctors applying for limited registration must have completed, overseas, an internship of at least twelve months' duration that is recognised as satisfactory by the GMC. The Council is, however, prepared to consider exemption on 'compassionate grounds' when the applicant is a political refugee or in a case of sickness within the immediate family of the applicant.

There is more than one route to limited registration, but the standard one for overseas doctors settling in the UK is through the PLAB test.

The PLAB test is a test of professional knowledge and competence and English proficiency conducted by the 'Professional and Linguistic Assessment Board'. The test, which is run on fourteen occasions during the year and lasts for three days, includes both medical and language components. The medical component comprises a multiple choice question examination, a projected material examination and a clinical problem solving examination as well as an oral examination during which candidates' linguistic ability is assessed in addition to their medical knowledge.

The language component of the PLAB test includes, in addition to oral assessment, a written English examination and a comprehension of spoken English examination in which candidates respond to items heard on tape. (The language component is under review.)

The PLAB test is very strict and the pass-rate is low. The rate of success is not more than 30 or 35 per cent. The number of attempts at the test by doctors who have taken it and failed it is being restricted according to a procedure governed by the severity with which a doctor fails the test.

A small industry has grown out of the doctors' attempts at the PLAB test. In 1989, the Professional and Linguistic Assessment Board pocketed £720,320 from the fees for tests. A number of expensive correspondence, evening and day courses for preparing for the PLAB test as well as a range of books, past test papers and even video cassettes have been marketed for doctors intending to take the test, without any visible improvement of the pass-rate.

There are other routes to limited registration which afford exemption from the PLAB test, but they are limited to doctors with a strong academic background – i.e. doctors holding registrable additional qualifications such as FRCS or MRCP (UK) are normally granted exemption. Finally, sponsored overseas doctors who come here for further training can, under certain circumstances, be exempted from passing the test.

Doctors not eligible for any kind of registration

Doctors not eligible for any kind of registration have two options:

1 They can obtain a 'primary qualification' from one of the non-university licensing bodies (the Examining Board in England, the Board of Management of the Scottish Triple Qualification, and the Worshipful Society of Apothecaries of London). Doctors, however, will only be allowed to take these professional examinations after completing, from the beginning, the full undergraduate curriculum. This means that doctors will have to seek a university qualification. However, in certain exceptional circumstances – such as refugee status – the bodies may consider, in consultation with the GMC, admission to the professional examinations. The doctor will then need an offer of adoption for training by a medical school of at least twelve months.

These adoption courses are very difficult to obtain, and

medical schools tend to reserve their few places to overseas doctors who are charged extremely high overseas student fees. WUS was recently involved in finding such an adoption course for one of its clients. We wrote to all medical schools in the UK, and there was only one medical school prepared to 'consider' an application.

2 They can, in the UK do at least part of a course leading to a degree in medicine; but it might be difficult to get a place if the student is over 30, and it is likely that s/he will have to do, at least, the full three-year clinical component of the course.

What can be done?

There is no question that professional bodies, such as the GMC, must ensure that practitioners meet a required standard of professional training, experience and behaviour. On the other hand, it should be accepted, as a matter of principle, that people settled here as refugees or immigrants have the right to practise their professions.

The rationale behind recognition procedures should be clearly spelled out and discussed and reviewed regularly. The professional bodies should not only be confined to setting up tests of standards in the shape of a single examination but should also establish procedures for reaching those standards, such as bridging courses or suitable training and guidance; the single test should, perhaps, be replaced by a fair, continuous and comprehensible assessment of the capabilities and standards of the individual. At the moment, it is voluntary organisations such as WUS (which do not get any credit or funding to do so) which are trying to fill the gap, giving appropriate information, giving small grants for paying for the PLAB test or the preparation courses for such tests, contacting medical schools and individuals for further support and guidance, etc.

(WUS 1990)

PROFESSIONAL REQUALIFICATIONS: LAWYERS

Background

Lawyers are divided into two categories: solicitors (also known as law agents in Scotland) and barristers (England and Wales) or advocates (Scotland). In England and Wales, each belongs to a professional body: the one for solicitors is the Law Society; for barristers, the Bar Council.

A solicitor's main areas of work are: conveyancing (buying and selling of freehold and leasehold property), probate (formulation of wills, their execution and the estate and property of the deceased), litigation, and business and commercial law. A solicitor serves his/her time as a student and then as a trainee solicitor (what used to be called an articled clerk) before being issued with a practising certificate from the Law Society.

The most important aspect of the work of a barrister/advocate is the presentation of a lay client's case before a court or tribunal. Barristers/advocates cannot work directly for a member of the public and must be engaged by solicitors for particular types of work. Their apprenticeship is served at the Inns of Court – there are four in London: Lincoln's Inn, Gray's Inn, Middle Temple and Inner Temple.

Recognition of qualifications (England and Wales)

Those with an overseas law degree are eligible to re-qualify in the UK as solicitors by passing a Common Professional Examination (CPE). According to the Law Society, passing the CPE is regarded as having completed 'the academic stage of training'. In order to be eligible, a person must

1 Hold a degree in law (other than an honorary degree) conferred by a university outside the UK and the Republic of Ireland.
2 Have been granted by the Society by virtue of the subjects passed in that degree exemption from two or more of the core subjects in a CPE. The applicant must attach evidence of having passed the subject (or subjects) equivalent to the core subjects in a CPE, and full details of the nature and scope of the subject from which exemption is sought should be attached to the application.

A person seeking to establish that s/he is an eligible student should apply to the Society for a Certificate of Eligibility.

Courses for the examination are held at the College of Law and at a number of polytechnics approved by the CPE Board, which consists of representatives of the Bar, the Law Society and law teachers. The teaching institutions set their own examinations for the papers in the same way as they would do for a law degree, but the CPE Board approves the syllabus and monitors the examinations. This is a one-year, full-time course. Attendance may not be necessary for those who qualify for four or five exemptions and only have one or two subjects to cover.

After passing the CPE, students attend another one-year course leading to the final examination. The final courses are held at the College of Law and at polytechnics approved by the Law Society. The final examination itself is set on the contents of the course and is conducted by the Law Society. Articles are served for two years, either before or after attending the final course and passing the final examination.

In the case of barristers, law graduates of overseas universities may be admitted to become members of an Inn of Court, if they

- obtain a degree in law which the Council of Legal Education considers a satisfactory equivalent of a UK degree and which it considers, in the individual case, a satisfactory equivalent of a IIii standard of a UK degree;
- satisfy the Council that s/he has a knowledge of two or more core subjects equivalent to that possessed by the holder of a UK law degree.

These persons are required to obtain a Certificate of Eligibility from the Council of Legal Education before applying to an Inn of Court, and show that they intend and will be able to practice at the Bar of England and Wales or use their qualification in the course of their profession in the UK and have Home Office permission to remain in the UK to do so.

The academic stage is followed by a vocational stage. This is completed by attending a full-time, one-year course at the Inns of Court School of Law. This stage includes the teaching of skills such as research, fact management, opinion writing, interviewing, negotiating, drafting, advocacy, as well as of legal knowledge. Presumably these skills are internationally required for lawyers whether from a Common Law background or not. After completing the academic and vocational stage a student is eligible to be called to the Bar and become a barrister, but may not practise in England and Wales until a further stage has been completed. This is *pupillage*, a twelve-month 'apprenticeship' which is generally served with one twelve-month or two six-month spells with a practising barrister. Another obligation over a two-year period after joining an Inn of Court is 'keeping terms', i.e. dining in the Inn of Court twenty-four times during the two-year period required for the vocational and pupillage stages.

It is possible, at the discretion of the General Council of the Bar, for barristers from overseas who have practised within a Common Law system for three years, to be allowed to practise in the UK without going through these stages.

Refugees with overseas legal qualifications might have particular difficulty with the requirement to produce transcripts of degree certificates and copies of syllabuses as they have often had to leave their countries without such documentation.

If there is too long a period (over seven years) between the academic and vocational stages, the academic qualification may be declared to be 'stale'.

Black access to the legal profession

The problem of access to the legal profession is not only one of securing qualifications or even measuring equivalences of qualifications.

Recent research, commissioned by the Law Society and the Bar Council, about racism and discrimination within the profession in the UK highlights the problems that would be faced by people trying to have overseas qualifications and experience recognised. On the other hand, the fact that these professional bodies have addressed the issue means that at least the problem is being admitted.

A Law Society survey in 1988 produced evidence that just over 1 per cent of solicitors were black, and that they mostly worked in small 'black' firms or in welfare/legal aid work. However, a positive trend is that 80 per cent of those black solicitors have been admitted since 1976, and at a faster rate in the past five years. In 1990 (white) women solicitors newly qualifying for the first time outnumbered white males, so some traditional images are slowly being broken down. Major problems seem to revolved around city firms' prejudices in giving articles to black solicitors.

A Bar Council survey on race within the profession also reveals evidence of major obstacles to advancement by black applicants for the profession, especially at the pupillage stage. For example, key characteristics taken into account when selecting pupils could have so many facial undertones – e.g. compatibility with other members of chambers, demeanour and turnout, ability to speak articulately.

References

Bar Council 1989 *Race Relations Survey* (Coopers & Lybrand), March.
Brunel University/CRE 1990 *Report*.
Council of Legal Education *Guidance on Completing Academic/Vocational Training* and *Consolidated Regulations*.
Law Society (1989) *The Race Report* (report of the Race Relations Committee), April.

Contacts

Both the Law Society and the Bar Council have Race Relations Committees which meet, and meet each other, regularly.

The Law Society has had a Minority Access to the Legal Profession Project which has funded a research project by Brunel University and CRE and has also funded an Ethnic Minorities Careers Officer (Mr G. Garvey).

They could be approached to fund part of the Overseas Qualifications project. Their telephone numbers are:- Law Society 071-242 1222; 0527-517 141 (Legal Education); Bar Council 071-242 0082; 071-404 5787 (Legal Education).

(WUS and Refugee Council 1990)

Chapter 5

APL and speakers of other languages and dialects

The question of language has already arisen in preceding chapters, in the context of racism and prejudice, and as one of the issues confronting people with qualifications from overseas. In Chapter 2 we mentioned the failure to recognise the value of an ability to communicate in more than one language, and the fact that accent or dialect and use of a language other than English can become the focus of prejudice. We will look at these issues further in this chapter. Linking in with this is the fact that many skills and abilities can be evidenced and demonstrated perfectly clearly in any language, so that the APL process can be a valuable means of gaining credit for those whose other skills exceed their skill in the use of English. At the same time it is not always made clear, in the case of vocational qualifications, what English language skills a candidate is expected to have. The guidelines and criteria for many vocational qualifications are unspecific as far as language is concerned, which can turn out to be either an advantage or a disadvantage for those advising and assessing and for candidates.

THE USE OF LANGUAGES OTHER THAN ENGLISH

Considerable importance has been attached to the development of children's mother tongue in schools in many European countries, particularly where there are large linguistic minorities and communities which have fought for the development of their languages themselves. It is generally recognised that language is part of identity, both for individuals and groups, and that it is important both psychologically and educationally to maintain language and culture. At the same time, Suzanne Romaine in *Bilingualism* points out that:

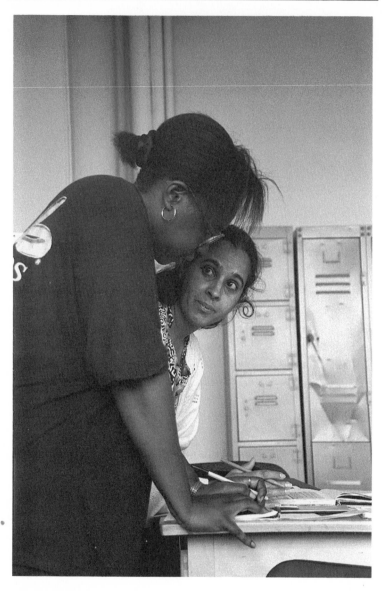

© Lenny Peters

Usually the more powerful groups in any society are able to force their language upon the less powerful . . . . .in Britain, the British child does not have to learn Punjabi or Welsh, but both these groups are expected to learn English.

(Romaine 1989)

The Welsh people have struggled long and hard to maintain and develop their language and establish its official use, and an indicator of their success is that the RSA now offers bilingual Welsh/English Diplomas in Administrative and Secretarial Procedures, and a bilingual Welsh/English Clerical Certificate. It is also preparing to offer Business Administration qualifications at NVQ Levels 1, 2 and 3 as bilingual Welsh/English schemes. It offers a Certificate in Business Language Competence in French, German, Spanish and Italian, but nothing in any of the languages spoken by many substantial communities in Britain. There does not appear to be any Examining and Validating body that offers bilingual certification in Gujerati, Urdu, Bengali, Turkish, or any of the other non-European languages in which people in Britain do business, publish newspapers, practise medicine or carry out other communal activities. The exception is one language option in GNVQs, which can apparently be gained in any language, provided there is someone available to assess it. However, large numbers of people function fruitfully in their daily lives, in paid or unpaid activity, often without using any English at all or only very limited English. Others function efficiently in two or more languages as a natural part of their activities.

In the preceding chapter we looked at some of the issues around recognition of professional qualifications gained overseas. Let us now consider the position of people with vocational skills and abilities who speak languages other than English. The NCVQ, in its note on *Access and Equal Opportunities in Relation to National Vocational Qualifications* (1988) makes no mention of language, so that decisions as to whether the language of a candidate is appropriate for the acquisition of a qualification are left to the discretion of the assessor. At the same time, BTEC and City and Guilds, in conjunction with NCVQ, have stated that language competence should match work role demands. This criterion raises infinite possibilities for the accreditation of competences in different language environments, and this has indeed taken place in a number of different circumstances, for example:

- Chinese chefs working in an environment where Cantonese is spoken have gained accreditation of units towards a City and Guilds qualification, which will be of considerable importance to them if they choose to go and work in other European countries.
- A Hindi/Punjabi speaking woman has gained accreditation of units towards Level 2 Business Administration NVQs for her work as a doctor's receptionist where she uses community languages most of the time.
- The organiser of clubs for elderly Gujerati speaking men and women has gained accreditation towards the RSA Advanced Diploma in the Organisation of Community Groups through her work, nearly all conducted through the medium of Gujerati.

In the second example the ability to speak more than one language is a considerable asset in the job; in the last one, it is essential for the success of the project. In these two cases the candidates were able to communicate in English as well as in their other languages whereas in the first example this was not necessarily the case. Some of the chefs spoke very little English indeed but it was possible to assess them through observation and with the help of staff who spoke English and Cantonese. In the case of assessment for candidates who speak little or no English, it is obviously desirable that the adviser and assessor speak a language in common with the candidate, or that good interpreting facilities are available.

Problems can arise with units such as Health and Safety. NCVQ nowhere states that candidates must understand Health and Safety regulations in English, yet many advisers and assessors expect candidates to be able to read difficult and lengthy Health and Safety documents without translation or explanation. Others consider an understanding of the regulations through the medium of another language, oral or written, acceptable. It has also been demonstrated, by an engineering lecturer, that awareness of Health and Safety regulations can be assessed practically, for example by the assessor setting up a machine incorrectly and instructing the candidate to prepare it for use, so that the candidate demonstrates knowledge by making the necessary adjustments.

The fact that these details around language and literacy are completely unspecified can work for or against candidates, depending on the awareness and attitudes of advisers and assessors. So, for example, one adviser might suggest that a candidate cannot apply for accreditation of a typing unit if she can only type in Bengali at the required speed. Another might check with the assessor that this was acceptable and ensure that the candidate gained credit for the unit. It would be preferable for criteria to be more specific if it is genuinely intended that vocational skills should be the target of assessment, rather than linguistic or literary skills. If accreditation of skills and abilities for people with restricted knowledge of English were more widespread it would enable a lot of people already working to gain units of accreditation and would also facilitate appropriate advice for those who have arrived recently in Britain, or are seeking education or training after time spent in the home, or in a community environment where English is not spoken. The hope is that NVQs will accredit skills which are not dependent on a high level of literacy, as distinct from academic qualifications for which sophisticated language use is a prerequisite. In this way they will constitute broadened opportunities, and a tangible outcome of the APL process, for people in or seeking to enter vocational fields.

Language and the Afro-Caribbean community

In *Language and Power* a student at a college in London is quoted as follows:

> When I arrived in England in the 1960s it was a cultural shock to me. I thought I spoke English when I arrived but I learnt I didn't. I was ridiculed and laughed at in school. Teachers said I was backward and uneducated because of my accent . . .
> (ILEA 1990)

The chapter goes on to say that although everyone agrees that a good command of Standard English is essential for success at school in Britain, it is debatable whether this can be achieved by suppressing the child's own language, and that Creole should be encouraged and developed alongside Standard English. It says:

> Most people from the Caribbean still continue to speak Creole in their homes and with their friends. Children born in Britain to Afro-Caribbean parents hear Creole spoken around them from an early age, as well as different varieties of English. They

usually grow up understanding and speaking a mixture of Creole, Standard English and the local variety of English.

(ILEA 1990)

Noyona Chanda of the Language and Literacy Unit suggests that this has resulted in the development of a kind of interlanguage, because of insufficient development in any of the three languages. The fact that Creole is not universally recognised as a language in its own right and taught as such would be a contributory factor, although the same phenomenon is described amongst Bengali youth growing up in Britain. What is certain is that due to these factors, coupled with poor educational provision in many inner city areas, a large number of young people are growing up with poor language skills, particularly as far as the written language is concerned. With high unemployment, especially among youth, this is another element in fostering feelings of alienation and lack of self-worth. Acquiring NVQs through the APL process, learning to evaluate and appreciate the skills that they have developed both in school and outside, can prove very worthwhile and act as a springboard to further education or training, with careful and well informed advice. A teacher in a comprehensive school in East London described how many of his pupils, often those with poor academic records in school, gained accreditation for units towards NVQs through evidence given by their Saturday job employers, who valued their contributions highly and helped them develop their skills in an environment where they did not feel that they were failures.

The language of competences and criteria

The skills of those involved in implementing the process are obviously a major factor in determining its appropriacy to the candidates, but there are two major constraints, as far as language is concerned, related to competence-based assessment:

1 The language in which the competences and criteria are formulated.
2 The implications contained in the competences and criteria with regard to language.

A readability survey conducted on the language of the competences and criteria for the LCCI Business Administration Level 2 NVQs showed a score of between fourteen and twenty. This puts the readability level at its highest beyond the level of newspapers such as the *Guardian or* the *Daily Telegraph*, and at its lowest higher than that of the tabloid press, which is usually estimated at between ten and twelve. To take an example, the performance criteria for Unit 10: Creating and Maintaining Business Relationships, read as follows:

- requests from colleagues within the jobholder's responsibility are actioned promptly and willingly, where possible
- essential information is passed on to colleagues promptly and accurately
- assistance, when required, is requested politely
- effective and mutually beneficial arrangements are made regarding division of work and joint responsibilities
- significant difficulties in working relationships are discussed, resolved or reported accurately to an appropriate authority.

Many people, whether or not Standard English is their medium of communication at home or elsewhere, would have some difficulties with this phraseology, and at the same time be perfectly capable of fulfilling all the criteria. In this way the language could actually hamper them in gaining accreditation for work they are doing, or have done in the past, and advisers may have to spend precious and expensive time going through criteria with candidates. Some of these criteria could be easily rephrased in more accessible language, for example:

- if other people at work ask you to do something which is part of your job you do it quickly and willingly if you can; or
- you agree to divide up the work and responsibility in a way that suits everyone.

An example of competences, from the RSA Advanced Diploma in the Organisation of Community Groups, reads as follows:

Unit 8   Maintain External Relations
8.1   Enable the group to establish a clear and consistent image
8.2   Represent the purposes and aims of the group externally
8.3   Speak in public about the group's activities or a particular aspect of the group's activities
8.4   Contact potential members of the group

Again, many people working in community groups will be

carrying out these activities extremely effectively, but might not express them in this way, at least not in English. Why not say:

8.1   Make sure the group becomes well known for what it does

8.4   Get in touch with people who might like to join

If there is a genuine commitment to greater accessibility to accreditation through these types of qualification it seems counter-productive to formulate the competences and criteria in language which in itself constitutes a barrier to potential candidates.

The second issue around the language of competences and criteria concerns the implications contained within them about a candidate's linguistic ability. We have already mentioned the fact that to gain NVQs the candidate is required to be competent in English to the standard required for employment in the UK. If we look more closely at some of the competences for qualifications such as City and Guilds 706/1 in Catering, we find that whilst the practical competences are quite clearly demonstrable without the use of language, under Inferred Knowledge it is stated that:

The candidate will be able to state, list, describe, identify or recognise the following:

1 The method of baking.
2 Fresh and convenience foods suitable for baking.
3 The effects of baking on the foods identified above.
4 The points associated with baking that require attention.
5 The techniques appropriate to different methods and applications.
6 The work necessary before, during and after baking.
7 The general rules for efficiency in baking.
8 The general safety rules for baking.

The question arises, is it acceptable, for example, to identify or recognise the effects of baking on foods without speaking English, or would it be considered necessary for employment purposes that the candidate have sufficient knowledge of the spoken language to explain them? Would candidates be required to read or write the general rules for efficiency in baking, or would an oral explanation be sufficient? This is not made clear and could obviously be the subject of negotiation with an assessor, but does this mean different outcomes with different assessors?

There seems no logical reason why people with poor English language or literacy skills should not gain credit for vocational competences, as long as they can prove their awareness of rules and regulations orally or practically. Likewise, if fluent written or spoken English is not a job requirement why should not people with limited English be accredited for vocational skills? This would be more likely to happen, though, if NCVQ were specific about the interpretation of competences and criteria. Two examples of mismatch between English language and skills are:

1 A woman from Sri Lanka with nine years experience of catering, through work as a cook in two different restaurants, in one case with supervisory responsibility, comes to college to get a City and Guilds 706 because she has been offered a job in Australia but the employer insists on a qualification. She can speak English but her reading and writing are weak.

2 A man newly arrived from Somalia enrols on a basic engineering course leading to City and Guilds 201, with English language support, because he does not know much English. It soon becomes apparent to the engineering staff that he has considerable experience and the engineering element of the course is far too easy for him. It transpires that he has completed part of a degree course and has worked as an automatic lathe setter in a factory and as a car mechanic in the army in Somalia.

These examples demonstrate the need for both careful bilingual counselling and ongoing language support for bilingual people seeking qualifications and progression. They highlight the fact that very often people who have recently arrived in Britain or who are not confident about their use of the English language will disregard their previous experience themselves, or find it disregarded by those reponsible for enrolling them on courses. In an article for *ALBSU News*, 'Assessment of Prior Learning: A Commonsense Approach for ABE and ESOL', Noyona Chanda stresses the prime importance for students of ABE and ESOL of 'becoming active learners: being able to have a clear idea of learning goals and strategies for learning that are based on analysis of all prior learning experiences' (Chanda 1990).

She suggests the following strategies for overcoming difficulty in communicating in English during the APL process:

1 Assessment of prior learning and purpose of assessment procedures could be explained in the student's first language
   (printed leaflet, interpretation facilities at interviews with educational guidance and advice workers, asking student to bring
   someone fluent in both first language and English to the very
   first session, etc.).
2 Students could be given time and a format for recording their
   learning history in whatever language they are comfortable in,
   and reference made to this record in ensuing discussions (written
   details are often easier to translate into another language,
   because the process of thinking about content has already been
   done).
3 The tutor could draw attention to the fact that use of first
   language by the student to recall, revise and absorb
   information is a resource in learning and could accelerate the
   process of becoming efficient in the use of English, by adopting
   a 'contrastive and comparative' strategy.

A positive outcome to the APL process is obviously always the
aim of those participating, but in the case of those who have been
transplanted to a new life and culture or had negative previous
experiences it is all the more important, as a positive statement of
achievement and an awareness raising of potential. However, if
candidates like those in the examples mentioned above are to be
able to follow on from their past attainment and reach future
goals the provision of ongoing language support is essential.
Language support is defined in the National Association of
Teachers of English and Community Languages to Adults/
Further Education Unit (NATECLA/FEU) document *Language in
Education* as: 'support for any students who wish to communicate
effectively in any subject, skill or learning situation, it can apply
equally to monolingual and bilingual students, to black students
and white students' (NATECLA/FEU 1989).
   The crucial importance of language, whether we are talking
about English for speakers of other languages or Standard
English for speakers of varieties or dialects, is that it confers
power. Whatever skills and abilities people have acquired and
however much they and others value their achievements, an
ability to operate in Standard English, when they choose and
when they consider it appropriate, can only add to the choices
available and the control they have over their own future direction.

It is therefore important that APL advisers are aware of the possibilities and make clear to candidates how they can improve their language skills, even if they can acquire accreditation without them. It is also important that institutions offering APL have flexible language support available, or can refer candidates to institutions which have, not only during the APL process but also in the institution as a whole. This can take a variety of forms depending on what is required and the resources available, such as:

- courses with integrated language support, where language is taught alongside other subjects
- general language only classes
- language classes for specific purposes
- language workshops.

In the two examples mentioned above, the Somali student enrolled on a course with integrated language support, whereas what he probably needed was language classes related to his specific subject, followed by entry to HE with ongoing support. The Sri Lankan woman would have benefited from a course leading to City and Guilds 706 with integrated language support if available or language classes for caterers. Obviously, it is often going to be difficult to find exactly what people require in the most convenient place but the responsibility must lie with advisers for finding the best possible solutions, otherwise there is always a danger of raising false hopes, which results in discouragement, quite the opposite outcome to that intended.

Working in a multilingual environment and APL

One way of approaching the issue of language with teaching staff who are working with NVQs is to get them to look at the criteria and competences they are concerned with in terms of the underlying linguistic demands they make on candidates for accreditation. In the following exercise for staff development, participants are asked to go through this process, in the hope that it will not only enable them to accredit more flexibly through separating language skills from practical skills, but also lead to an understanding of the kinds of difficulties speakers of other languages might have in a practical situation and of how lecturers can facilitate their learning by using strategies which do not make linguistic demands.

EXERCISE

As we have seen, language awareness is a central element in making the APL process a powerful tool for extending equality of opportunity. Because of this the following exercise should be done with all staff. Participants are asked to look at a list of competences and discuss what skills they are designed to assess. They are then asked to discuss what language skills a candidate would need in order to demonstrate competence. Finally, they are asked to look at a CV and decide which competences the person concerned might wish to claim credit for.

Multicultural staff development

Workshop: the implication of working in a multilingual environment for the assessment and accreditation of prior learning.
   Group task:

1 Look at the list of competences you have been given and discuss and decide what it is the different competences are designed to assess, e.g. practical skills, knowledge of theory, background reading, etc.
2 Look again at the list of competences and discuss and decide what language skills a person would need to demonstrate in each of them, e.g. oral fluency in English/mother tongue, literacy in English/mother tongue, writing skills in English/mother tongue, or none of these.
3 Look at the CV you have been given and assess which of the competences this person could probably be accredited for.

Please mark your conclusions on the list which follows the exercise material (p. 101).

CURRICULUM VITAE

Name   Abdullah Mohammed

Address   144 Plaistow Road, Stratford, London E15

Date of birth   27 July 1960

Education   1971–6 Sheikh Basheir Secondary School, Mogadishu Secondary School Leaving Certificate.
1976–9 Cismane Hargse College, Mogadishu University Entrance Science and French.
1988–90 University of Mohammed, Morroco French and Architecture. Completed two units including technical drawing.

Work   1979–81 Automatic Lathe Setter in factory
1981–3 Made furniture and toys in a small co-operative.
1984–7 Military Service. Received training in car mechanics.

Note   Abdullah came to Britain as a refugee and found a place on an ESOL/Engineering course at the College. The engineering part of the course at the College. The engineering part of the course aimed for accreditation at NVQ Level 1, City and Guilds 201 Engineering. Although Abdullah's English, particularly his oral ability, is poor, it became obvious to the vocational lecturers that the engineering element of the course was far too easy for him.

Basic competence in removing material

On award of this unit, the candidate will have demonstrated the ability to remove material during turning, sawing, drilling and milling operations, working to given drawings.

Element of competence 1

Complete basic turning operations using a centre lathe and wood-turning lathe.

Performance criteria

1 Correct machine tool identified.
2 Correct tools used.
3 Feeds and speeds correctly calculated.
4 Component diameters meet specification.
5 Tolerance + – 0.01mm on diameter.
6 To within 1.6 micro-metres surface roughness.
7 Work completed safely and within prescribed time parameters.

Element of competence 2

Mill a flat or slot on:

• Horizontal milling machine using slab mill, slitting saw, slotting cutter, side and face cutter.
• Vertical milling machine using face mill, end mill, two fluted slot drill.

Performance criteria

1 Correct machine tool identified.
2 Correct tools chosen.
3 Feeds and speeds calculated correctly.
4 Work secured safely.
5 Tolerance + – 0.0.1mm, 1.6 micro-metres surface roughness.
6 Component meets specification.
7 Work completed safely and within prescribed time parameters.

Element of competence 3

Drill and ream a hole, spotface, counterbone, countersink.

Performance criteria

1 Correct tools chosen.
2 Feeds and speeds correctly calculated.
3 Work secured safely.
4 Work diameter to acceptable standards and depth.
5 Surface finish to 1.6 micro-metres.
6 Work completed safely and within prescribed time parameters.

Element of competence 4

Shape a flat surface horizontal and vertical, two flat surfaces at 90 degrees to each other, using single point cutting tools.

Performance criteria

1 Feeds and speeds correctly chosen.
2 Surface finish to 1.6 micro-metres, tolerance + − − 0.01mm
3 Work correctly secured in vice/table.
4 Work completed safely and within prescribed time parameters.

Element of competence 5

Cut to length using mechanical hacksaw.

Performance criteria

1 Component length + − 1.0mm.
2 Work completed safely.

The following knowledge (in this unit) can be inferred from performance

Demonstrated in unit nos

1 Interpretation of drawings.
2 Identification and selection of machine tools and processes.
3 Support and restraint of cutting tools and work against cutting forces.
4 Correct use of inspection equipment.
5 Application of Health and Safety at Work act and other relevant legislation.

The following knowledge (in this unit) cannot be inferred from performance

Demonstrated in unit nos

1 The factors affecting the penetration of the cutting edge.
2 The angles of a wedge-shaped cutting tool and the terminology.
3 The relationship between the depth of cut and the feed rate in the material removal process.

Below is a multiple-choice test designed to test knowledge.

BASIC COMPETENCE IN MOVING LOADS

Please answer A, B, C or D in the boxes

(6) When slinging, a bowline is used to:

☐ Y/N

A prevent the load from tightening the loop

B join ropes of equal thickness

C fasten a rope to a sling

D prevent a sling slipping off the crane hook

---

(7) Which one of the following is used in a hydraulic system to transmit movement?

☐ Y/N

A oil

B grease

C gas

D solvent

---

(8) Lifting gear powered by compressed air is classified as:

☐ Y/N

A aerated

B hydraulic

C pneumatic

D hydrogas

CURRICULUM VITAE

Name   Raúl Gomez

Nationality   Guatemalan

Date of birth   29 May 1956

Marital status   Married

Address   500 Romford Road, London E1

Permanent address   Apartado Postal 5429,
                            San José, Costa Rica,
                            Central America

Studies

Teacher of Urban Primary Education
Escuela Normal Central para Varones
Guatemala, 1976.

Studies in Agricultural Sciences
University of San Carlos
Guatemala, 1978–80.

Management Computing
National School of Electronic Computing
San José, Costa Rica, 1986–8.

Courses and Seminars

'An Introduction to the Data Electronic Processing'
International Institute of Computing Studies
Guatemala, 1976.

'Programming in RPG I and RPG II'
International Institute of Computing Studies
Guatemala, 1976.

'I and II Congress of Academic Reorganization
    of the Agronomy Faculty'
University of San Carlos
Guatemala, 1976 and 1980

'Program of Teaching Training'
Institute of Research and Educative Improvement
University of San Carlos
Guatemala, 1980.

'First Seminar on the Social Sciences and the Health Sciences
   in the Curriculum of the University of San Carlos'
University of San Carlos
Guatemala, 1980.

'Seminar of Information Centres' Management'
Latin American Economic System (SELA)
Managua, Nicaragua, 1980.

'Basic Course of Information'
Centre of Professional Updating
Managua, Nicaragua, 1981.

'Course of Structured Design of Information Systems'
Centre of Professional Updating
San José, Costa Rica, 1986.

'Fifth Annual Seminar of Microcomputers: New Trends
   and Technologies'
Centre of Professional Updating
San José, Costa Rica, 1986.

'Curse Uses of the Non-Numerical Databases Manager
   MICRO-CDS/ISIS'
Central American Universities Council (CSUCA)
San José, Costa Rica, 1987.

Workshop: 'Telecommunications for Central America'
Regional Council of Social Research
San José, Costa Rica, 1987.

Work Experience

Member of the Reorganization Commission of the
   Agronomy Faculty
University of San Carlos
Guatemala, 1978–80.

Assistant Teacher of General Biology
Agronomy Faculty, University of San Carlos
Guatemala, 1980

Coordinator of the Organizer Commission of the
  'First University Seminar on Science and Technology'
University of San Carlos
Guatemala, 1980.

Analyst of Documents
Information Centre and Library
Ministry of Housing and Human Settlements
Managua, Nicaragua, 1981.

Research Assistant
Latin American Faculty of Social Science (FLACSO)
San José, Costa Rica, 1985–6.

Award holder of the Programme of Research Grants of Central
American Universities Council (CSUCA) – Latin American
Faculty of Social Sciences (FLACSO) – Central American
Institute of Public Administration (ICAP); with the research
'The San José, Costa Rica, 1985.

Assistant Teacher of the Course 'Information Systems
  and Computing'
Diploma in International Relations
Latin American Faculty of Social Sciences (FLACSO)
San José, Costa Rica, 1987.

Founder and First Director of the Computer Centre
Latin American Faculty of Social Sciences (FLACSO)
San José, Costa Rica, 1986.

Specific works

Analysis, Design and Management of the Data Bank 'Figures
of Central America'.

Analysis, Design and Management of the Data Base
'Publications of the Latin American Faculty of Social Sciences'.

Analysis, Design and Management of the Data Bank on the
Peace Plan Esquipulas II.

Editor of the 'Papers of Social Sciences'
Latin American Faculty of Social Sciences (FLACSO)
San José, Costa Rica, May–October 1988.

Computing Adviser
Central American Association of Relatives of Disappear Persons
San José, Costa Rica, 1988.

Publications

Base de Datos Indicadores de Centroamérica: Guía de Consulta,
(Database Figures of Central America: A Guide to Query), San
José, Costa Rica, FLACSO, 1986.

'Ordenadores y Ciencias Sociales' (Microcomputers and Social
Science), *Papers of Social Science*, San José, Costa Rica, FLACSO,
1989. In process.

Processing of information and test of the text publications

Gallardo, Maria Eugenia y Roberto Lopez. *Centroamérica: la
Crisis en cifras* (Central America: The Crises in Figures), San
José, Costa Rica, FLACSO-IICA, 1986. 260 pages.

FLACSO (Latin American Faculty of Social Sciences), *FLACSO:
Catálogo de Publicaciones 1982–1986* (FLACSO: Catalog of
Publications 1982–1986), San José, Costa Rica, FLACSO, 1987.
320 pages.

Papers of Social Sciences. Latin American Faculty of Social
Sciences, San José, Costa Rica, 1987–8.

Latin American Faculty of Social Sciences – Central American
Universities Council – The Peace University (FLACSO-CSUCA-
UPAZ). *I y II Informe Blanco sobre el cumplimiento del Plan de Paz
'Esquipulas II'* (First and Second White Paper on the Achieve-
ment of the Peace Plan 'Esquipulas II'), San José, Costa Rica,
FLACSO-CSUCA-UPAZ, 1988 (Spanish and English versions).
180 and 240 pages.

Asociación Centro Americana de Familiares de Detenidos
Desaparecidos (Central American Association of Relatives of
Disappear Persons), *Guatemala, desaparecidos* (Disappear
Persons in Guatemala), San José, Costa Rica, ACAFADE, 1988.

London, April 1989

Note: Raúl's written English is poor, although his oral skill is of inter-
mediate standard.

Checklist of computing competences for GCLI 726

Introductory unit

- Define a computer system and its components.
- Identify and explain the different types of computer memory and secondary storage.
- Explain the terms on-line, real-time and batch processing.
- Describe the types of available input and output devices.
- Explain the use of different types of networks in computer communication.
- Describe the different levels of programming languages; list their characteristics, advantages and disadvantages.
- Explain the use of compilers, assemblers and interpreters in program translation.
- Identify different types of software.

COBOL programming

- Design, code and document a program in COBOL.
- Explain the handling of records and files in programming.

Spreadsheets

- Explain the use of a spreadsheet and the basic terms associated with it.
- Set up a spreadsheet.
- Manipulate a spreadsheet by using commands for amending the format of cells, editing data, inserting and deleting rows and columns and changing the existing settings.
- Use block commands in a spreadsheet; define, copy and delete a block.
- Use a spreadsheet to perform a range of mathematical functions such as adding, subtracting, dividing, multiplying, summing and averaging values.
- Identify potential applications which include numerical analyses, financial and non-financial uses of spreadsheets.

Databases

- Identify the characteristics and uses of different filing systems.
- ·Define the term database and explain its uses and advantages over other filing systems.

- Set up a database.
- Manipulate a database by performing operations such as adding, changing, deleting and sorting records as well as searching the database. .
- Identify the features and requirements of database packages.

Word-processing

- Describe the components that make up a word-processor.
- Identify the advantages of word-processing and outline the existing word-processing facilities available.
- Prepare a word-processed document using appropriate layout and presentation techniques.

Note: At the time of writing Competences for Computing had yet to be devised.

CURRICULUM VITAE

Name	Verny Mageswaran	
Address	39 Burton House, Swaine Road, London E7	
Date of birth	5 April 1956	
Education	1966–73	Chundikuli Girls College, Jafna, Sri Lanka
Employment	1974–6	Altat Stores Shop Assistant
	1977–81	Shari Curry House Cook
	1984–	Sagore Restaurant Cook
Further education	1984–5	ESOL Beginners Course PT
	1989–	CGLI 706/1 Course.

Note

Although Verny had no formal training, she worked as the main cook supervising two other workers in the Sagore Restaurant in Forest Gate. She has two children to support. Her marriage ended in 1988, and she is determined to maintain her living standards. She has recently been offered a good position in Australia, working for a construction firm, which would provide accommodation and an excellent salary. She will not be allowed to take up the job unless she can show a qualification to prove that she is a skilled cook. Accreditation of Prior Learning for the CGLI 706 series would be the quickest way of obtaining the necessary qualification. However, Verny's English is poor, particularly her reading and writing.

Safe hygiene practices

Underpinning knowledge – not inferred from
performance

The candidate will be able to list, state or be able to
recognise the following:

1 The law in regard to hygiene in catering:
   (a) the legal regulations applicable to food premises
       The Food Act 1984
       Food and Drugs – (Control of Food Premises
       Act 1976)
       Food Hygiene Regulations 1970
       Material and Articles – (in contact with Food –
       1978 Food Hygiene – (Market Stalls and
       Delivery Vehicles) 1966;
   (b) the role of the Environmental Health Officer
       and his powers.
2 The human and environmental conditions that can
   lead to food poisoning and the methods of prevention.
3 The means and necessity to develop positive
   personal attitudes to hygiene:
   (a) to work and act in a hygienic manner to
       protect self and others;
   (b) the dangers that can occur;
       what protection is available;
       how to reduce the risk of food poisoning.
4 Hygienic use of equipment/utensils and the
   prevention of cross contamination:
   (a) hygienic working practices and handling of
       equipment;
   (b) hygienic procedures for cleaning, maintaining,
       inspecting and storing equipment/utensils.
5 Hygienic handling of food during storage,
   preparation, cooking and serving:
   (a) how food may be contaminated;
   (b) dangers of cross contamination between
       cooked and uncooked foods;

Demonstrated
in unit nos

    (c) proper thawing of frozen food (where
         applicable) before cooking;
    (d) correct temperatures for cooking and reheating
         food;
    (e) the dangers relating to reheating foods;
    (f) storage of food and disposal of waste.
6 General rules for the observation of sale hygiene
   practices in catering:
    (a) maintain personal hygiene;
    (b) work hygienically;
    (c) handle foods/food products hygienically;
    (d) follow correct cleaning procedures;
    (e) report any symptoms of illness.

Unit title: Baking

On the award of this unit the candidate will have demonstrated
the ability to bake a range of products including basic flour
products including sweet and savoury items, milk and egg
custard based products, fruit and potato products, with special
regard to Health, Safety and Hygiene.

Element of competence 1

Plan and prepare to bake

1 Ingredients of the correct quality, type and quantity assembled
   and prepared in the required form.
2 Equipment and utensils of the correct type and size selected
   and prepared.
3 Oven preheated to correct temperature and prepared for use.

Element of competence 2

Cook food by baking

1 Food inserted at the correct position in preheated oven.
2 Appropriate cooking temperature maintained or adjusted
   throughout the cooking time.
3 Cooking time suitable to achieve the correct texture, colour,
   appearance.

4 On completion of cooking the food removed from the heat source and treated appropriately for service.
5 Equipment and utensils cleaned and stored.
6 During the cooking process the candidate maintains a smart appearance, good personal and food hygiene and good working practices.

Inferred knowledge

The candidate will be able to state, list, describe, identify or recognise the following:

1 The methods of baking.
2 Fresh and convenience foods suitable for baking.
3 The effects of baking on the foods identified above.
4 The points associated with baking that require attention.
5 The techniques appropriate to different methods and applications.
6 The work necessary before, during and after baking.
7 The general rules for efficiency in baking.
8 The general safety rules for baking.

	Demonstrated in unit nos
Underpinning knowledge not inferred from performance	
The candidate will be able to list, state or be able to recognise the following:	
1 Baking: as the cooking of prepared foods or food items by convected dry heat in an oven.	
2 The purpose of baking: (a) to make food digestible, palatable and safer to eat; (b) to produce a desired flavour, colour, texture and eating quality.	
3 The advantages of baking: (a) effective manual/automatic control of temperature; (b) loading, access and removal of items is straight-forward; (c) products cooked uniformly in specially designed ovens.	

4 Identify the appropriate equipment and describe its routine care and method of inspection before and after use.
  (a) equipment
      pastry oven
      general purpose oven ranges
      forced air convection ovens
      small equipment and utensils;
  (b) routine care
      cleaning
      handling
      storage;
  (c) method of inspection
      check cleanliness
      check condition for safe use
      report any faults.

WORKSHEET

Competence number	What is being assessed?	Language skills needed	Can this person be accredited?
1			
2			
3			
4			
5			
6			
7			
8			
9			
10			
11			
12			
13			
14			
15			
16			
17			
18			
19			
20			
21			
22			
23			
24			

Chapter 6

People with disabilities

In Chapter 1 we mentioned that there are six and a quarter million people with disabilities in this country, 200,000 of whom are currently school pupils. Although the 1981 Education Act endorsed the principle that disabled children should be educated alongside non-disabled children, this is still the exception rather than the norm, with only one in five being educated in the same schools as other children. People with learning difficulties have only been included in education officially since the 1971 Education Act, having formerly been deemed ineducable. The determination of parents is often a major factor affecting where a child with disabilities is educated, with only those who are prepared to put up a fight succeeding in getting places for their children in the mainstream. Sometimes people with disabilities are protected and sheltered in such a way as to prevent them from realising their full potential. Children and young people who do get into schools and colleges often face enormous physical and psychological difficulties where insufficient thought or funding has gone into provision for their support and welfare in educational establishments. Many people with disabilities spend long periods of their lives in homes, hospitals or day centres. In a society which often has low expectations of their potential and in which little is done to bring down the barriers they face to participation in the broader community, APL can prove a crucial starting-point for people with disabilities in validating past experience positively, and opening up routes to qualifications and employment.

© Lenny Peters

THE EXPERIENCE OF PEOPLE WITH DISABILITIES

The British Council of Organisations of Disabled People (BCODP), and following them, the Disabled Persons International (DPI), recognised by the United Nations as the representative body of people with disabilities internationally, and which stands for only those organisations which have at least 51 per cent disabled people on their controlling committee, have adopted the following definitions of impairment and disability:

> Impairment – lacking part or all of a limb, or having a defective limb, organ or mechanism of the body.

> Disability – the disadvantage or restriction of activity caused by a contemporary social organisation which takes little or no account of people who have physical impairments and thus excludes them from participation in the mainstream of social activities – physical disability is therefore a particular form of social oppression.

There is no doubt that discrimination against people with disabilities is inherent in the institutions of our society and that as a result of this people with disabilities have a lower standard of living than the majority of the community. People with disabilities are three times more likely to be unemployed than those who are not disabled and, as we saw in Chapter 1, disability is a significant factor in duration of unemployment. In addition to this, if they are working, people with disabilities are more likely to find themselves in low-paid, low-status jobs, with poor conditions and little security. The Employment Quota Scheme introduced in 1944 to ensure that all employers gave opportunities to people with disabilities has been largely disregarded, with open discrimination taking place in the majority of workplaces. This discrimination also operates across the board in post-16 educational establishments, despite, ironically, the most significant factor in increasing access for students of all needs and abilities being the current demographic trends, which cause post-16 institutions to cast the recruitment net wider in the face of diminishing numbers.

There are two major effects of institutionalised discrimination against people with disabilities in our society. One is the fact that they are frequently physically marginalised, through lack of access or facilities in buildings, transport and physical support.

The other is the resulting low expectation they may have of themselves, brought about by the low expectations society has of them, which is reflected in the attitudes of institutions and individuals as well as in the media.

Tanni Grey, 22-year-old British and world record holder for women's wheelchair racing, describes in an article in the *Guardian* (10 April 1992) how as a Loughborough University student she was not welcomed by the athletics club, and was only given a key to the running track after winning a bronze medal at the Seoul Paralympics.

Richard Rieser, a teacher in a comprehensive school who has a physical disability says: 'I have had to develop my awareness of myself in order to reject the view of myself I have internalised from society' (Rieser 1992).

These are examples of people who have determined themselves what they could or could not do, rather than letting society be the determiner. The social model of disability puts forward the view that 'It is the posture of society at large that constitutes the most disabling part of being disabled and not the physical effects of whatever condition we may have.'

THE ROLE OF APL

Does APL have a role to play in enabling people with disabilities to decide what they can or cannot do, and in changing their status of receivers into one of pro-active members of society?

There are two factors which suggest that APL is of particular relevance to people with disabilities. The first is that their learning will often have taken place or be taking place differently from that of others, and almost certainly in a setting with lower status than others, because of the way society is organised. Many will have been educated separately in special schools or hospital schools. They will often have been separated from their peer group, giving disabled people a different view of what is the norm and depriving non-disabled people of the opportunity to learn about and celebrate the different people in society, and thereby impoverishing the experience of all. Schooling, for people with disabilities, may have been interrupted by ill health or treatment or by the lack of suitable provision in an area, necessitating the uprooting of families. Lack of transport or inefficient transport systems may also have resulted in disrupted attendance. People with disabilities settling in this country as adults may not have had any formal schooling in their country of origin. Factors of race and class come into play. Those who are speakers of other languages or dialects may have a double disadvantage due to having had part of their education in a different language and system, or gaps in their education due to moving or to lack of facilities in their country of origin. Those who come from working-class families with a history of work in manual occupations have greater barriers to surmount to become qualified. As a result of these factors age may not be a useful guide to the level of education attained. People with disabilities may need to work more slowly or in short bursts. Their difficulties may have been compounded if, for example, they have both physical and learning difficulties, such as poor verbal skills and lack of memory, which require learning to take place in smaller groups with more structure and support.

The second important factor is that because learning has taken place in different circumstances the achievements of people with disabilities may not have been recorded. There is a trend nationally to integrate students with disabilities in schools and for all school leavers to have records of achievement. However, this is not yet a reality everywhere and people who have studied in segregated education are far less likely to have had access to accreditation. Because of this, when students arrive in post-16 education they may be placed on courses which put them through things they have done before. Many are so delighted to receive any education at all that they are totally uncritical consumers and do not readily disclose their existing skills, experience and achievements in case they lose their opportunities. People who have spent long periods of time in day centres or long stay hospitals will often have had considerable work experience and acquired a broad range of skills which have not been credited. As the government policy of moving people with disabilities out of hospitals into the community starts to take effect people are at the same time acquiring new skills and perceiving the need to have their existing skills recognised so that they can play a fuller part in the life of the community at large. If this does not happen they can find themselves trapped in a routine at a day centre with no prospect of change in the future.

People who have become disabled after working in manual occupations and are no longer able to continue in their job because of their disability, may have considerable skills which have not been accredited, or which could be used differently. A mechanic, for example, disabled as a result of an accident says: 'I can't do the job any more but I could teach it.'

Most people who were in good manual jobs before becoming disabled are not offered the opportunity to retrain. An HGV driver who contracted MS now spends his days watching television. These people face a total devaluing of their lives which does not necessarily take place with people in the professions. Musicians like Itzak Pehrlman or Stevie Wonder, teachers, architects, academics like Stephen Hawking, politicians like David Blunkett or Jack Ashley are often able to carry on in their chosen career in spite of restrictions, precisely because they are qualified, their skills are recognised and valued. The psychological blow of no longer being able to do what you were once good at can be considerably lessened by the process of valuing what you did achieve and working out how you can build on that to achieve more in the future.

How can APL be implemented?

The APL process, as previously stated, needs to be seen primarily as part of a college-wide admissions procedure including assessment and guidance, but also leading towards the negotiation of a programme of study and the appropriate support for the student to carry out that programme. This is particularly important for students with disabilities, as going through the process of working out progression routes for future learning will be extremely disillusioning if the necessary resources to support learning are not going to be made available.

Stages in the process of APL

Access

The first barriers to be overcome are the physical barriers to access. It is, of course, possible to run groups or individual sessions for APL in day centres, homes or hospitals but if APL is seen to be a step towards further study or employment, a step into a wider world, it could be appropriate to start the process by bringing people into a new environment. The importance for people with disabilities, both of getting together with other people with disabilities in an atmosphere of mutual exchange and support, and of claiming access to an environment hitherto closed to them, has been recognised. 'What is infinitely preferable to people battling with the world alone . . . is drawing disabled individuals into some kind of a forum to exchange support and ideas', says Micheline Mason, writing about the Disability Movement (Mason 1992).

The first stage will therefore be:

- choice of a venue accessible to people with disabilities
- allocation of resources for transport to and from the venue
- distribution of information to people's homes, hospitals, day centres or residential homes – information may need to be translated into languages spoken in the community, and into braille or recorded on tape for blind people, and should explain clearly and simply what the programme is about.
- follow up of information by visits to groups or individuals for further explanations

Once the members of the group have been identified it will be possible to identify any other needs that will arise in terms of support, such as a sign language interpreter for deaf people, language and literacy support, extra support for people with learning difficulties and any special equipment needed, such as attachments for IT equipment. The timing of the group will also have to take into account the transport arrangements of students and childcare arrangements where a crèche is not available. Women with disabilities are less likely to take up education and employment opportunities than men so it is important to ensure that no extra barriers stand in their way.

A group working together for the purpose of APL may not consist exclusively of people with disabilities and may include people with a range of different disabilities. On the other hand, it may be more appropriate or practical to introduce the APL process with an existing group as part of their course of study. Both these approaches have worked successfully. Students may prefer to go through the process very much on an individual basis, but there are considerable advantages to be gained from working as a group, in terms of mutual support and sharing of experiences.

A student on a portfolio preparation course says: 'Learning through the experience of listening and communication with the participants in the group was probably the most important thing I got from the course.'

The group has a key role to play in validating the experience of participants who have had low expectations of themselves through always having been told what to do, and through others' low expectations of their abilities. Through the APL process they can start to gain independence by valuing their past and taking responsibility for planning their future.

Identifying and reflecting on learning experiences

Most reports of work on APL quote examples of students discounting their experience as too trivial to report or to discuss. This seems to be a common experience with women and even more so with many people with disabilities, who may never have been encouraged to think of themselves as employable, even though they may actually have carried out jobs in the institutions which they have lived in or attended on a daily basis. Patients in long stay hospitals may have worked for years doing cleaning and catering jobs and people in day centres have often done piece work, packing or other manual jobs. In addition, all people with disabilities have the valuable experience of having that disability and thus being in a position to understand and help other people practically, by writing about it, or by running discussion or support groups or awareness training. Many people with disabilities will have been involved in voluntary organisations, in either a paid or unpaid capacity. Others will have run a home, brought up a family, cooked, shopped and organised in the same way as any other person occupied in unpaid work in the home. People who live in sheltered communities may well be involved in committees and in the general running of the organisation.

Advocates and counsellors involved in facilitating groups including people with disabilities will need particular skills and experience to assist in the valuing of their experience. Advocates who have the experience of a disability themselves will often have a particularly relevant perspective to offer. Skills in confidence building will obviously also be crucial to the process. Equally, discussion between advocate and assessor will be essential.

Claiming competence

Once the stage of reflection on experience has been gone through, either collectively or individually, those involved will have some idea of what evidence it will be possible to collect and what competences could, as a result, be claimed. This is a key stage, particularly where experience has been gained in an unorthodox fashion. The way competences have been constructed may in itself constitute a barrier to the acquisition of that competence. There may be an underlying assumption, for example, that a deaf or hearing impaired person will not be able to carry out reception duties, or a blind person to achieve competence at filing. The National Council for Vocational Qualifications (NCVQ) stipulates in its Information Leaflet No.3 on Access and Equal Opportunities:

> that arrangements be made for assessing candidates with special needs defined as including people with physical or sensory disabilities or learning difficulties who may require support to undertake assessment. Such support could include physical, mechanical or technical aids, extra time for assessment, or specially devised or adapted methods of assessment.
>
> (NCVQ 1988)

The council is clear that the way in which a competence is demonstrated is flexible, so that demonstration can take place in whatever situation the activity is normally carried out, and that 'Any valid method of assessment which provides evidence that competence has been achieved to the specified standard is permissible' (ibid.).

The Council's leaflet quotes as examples the use of oral questions as opposed to written ones and the use of mechanical aids such as typewriters or tape recorders, and goes on to say that:

> Such changes will normally need to be approved by the relevant awarding body, but NCVQ will be encouraging awarding bodies to be flexible in tolerating alternative assessment methods provided this does not result in changes in the performance criteria.
>
> (ibid.)

This notion of flexible assessment methods for NVQs is obviously of key importance in the APL process for people with disabilities, and provides enormous potential for the accreditation of a wide range of experience gained in 'purposeful activity with critical outcomes' (the NCVQ definition of work). Assessment for APL is always individualised and it is the assessor's responsibility to come up with the appropriate assessment for the standard, bearing in mind the requirements of the candidate. There is a big responsibility here both with regard to the fulfilment of the hopes of those participating in the process and with regard to the maintenance of standards and the value of the qualifications. It may be that the counsellor and candidate agree that the candidate is not ready for accreditation, in which case advice will need to be given on further training or study, accessible to the student and with the necessary support available. Even if accreditation is not achieved as a result of an APL programme the benefits can be enormous in terms of increased confidence and the opening up of access routes through dissemination of information, and practical measures such as relocating courses in accessible venues or providing transport.

In an open learning project run in the London Borough of Waltham Forest for people with disabilities, with the aim of providing educational counselling and helping students to progress, five of the six students progressed to other activities, in spite of difficulties with transport and facilities, such as lifts, and financial problems. In this instance both the importance of the group approach, as opposed to individual counselling, and the importance of contact with non-disabled people were emphasised.

If students are seeking accreditation through NVQs the competences will be listed for them. It will be the responsibility of the tutor or counsellor to ensure that the awarding body is in agreement with any special arrangements which need to be made for assessment, and that the assessor has had appropriate awareness training. Skilled interpretation of the implications of competence statements may be needed. We have already mentioned the use of oral skills as opposed to written skills, and the reverse may also be appropriate. A candidate who cannot communicate orally may be able to demonstrate a range of practical skills. If we take the example of the description of a CGLI Catering unit:

> On the award of this unit the candidate will have demonstrated the ability to bake a range of products including basic flour products including sweet and savoury items, milk and

egg custard based products, fruit and potato products, with special regard to Health, Safety and Hygiene.

(CGLI)

These abilities could all be demonstrated in the home, in a practical classroom, in a workplace or by the use of photographs. Tutors will have the responsibility of ensuring that students have the opportunity to demonstrate their skills in a safe and reassuring environment. The Equal Opportunities policy of the CGLI allows for the possibility of assessment in the candidate's home and it is also possible to arrange this in a day centre or simulated work environment.

Students seeking APL may not be following the route of NVQs, either because the area in which they wish to demonstrate competence is not covered by NVQs, or because they are seeking APL as a means of access to higher education, or for staff development purposes. In the absence of predetermined competence statements students and tutors will be involved in the drafting of competence statements to fit the experiences they have analysed, with a view to identifying transferable skills. People with disabilities may have developed particular skills with regard to investigating, planning, organising and negotiating because of the practical difficulties they often face. If they have spent time in institutions they may have developed group skills, they may have been involved in voluntary organisations or have a highly developed interest in a particular area of study without having obtained any qualifications. The preparation of a portfolio by the students, over a period of time, will be a rewarding process and provide valuable and lasting evidence of their abilities. Students will need plenty of time to build portfolios and at the same time develop the skills to produce a well laid out and presented record of their past achievement. The portfolio will be evidence that students can take to interviews and use as a means of presenting themselves and giving themselves confidence. It may prove the key to access to further study or gain them credits on courses.

Further support

If students do get accepted on to courses after APL it is essential that arrangements for on-going support are investigated and the facilities in the educational establishment are checked out before-hand. It is unfortunately not uncommon for students to arrive in polytechnics or universities to find that nobody has taken responsibility for ensuring that the necessary facilities are available, even basics such as ramps and lifts, or tape recording facilities for blind people and signers for those who are deaf or hearing impaired. There are access funds available to students in higher education which are not available in further education. Not all institutions are aware, for example, that students with dyslexia can claim funding for a word processor from social services as well as having the right to special conditions for examinations. APL counsellors will need to take responsibility for ensuring that the needs of those who progress through the process are recognised and catered for and that the process is seen as a part of a more generalised opening up of educational establishments. A statement from the Open University guidelines on dyslexia might be applicable to disabilities and learning difficulties as a whole: 'the single most helpful aspect is recognition by the student and staff' (Open University).

If staff and students recognise the validity of the needs of people with disabilities or learning difficulties and the duty of the institution to cater for those needs, just as it does for the needs of all the other students, half the battle is won. Staff development and awareness training is therefore a key factor, and we give a few suggestions in the following exercises, followed by an example of information put out by the disability support team in one college.

EXERCISES

Disability and the individual

Participants divide into pairs. Each pair is asked to consider a particular physical disability such as blindness, impairment of hearing, paraplegia, epilepsy, and assess how it would affect the way they function in their daily lives, at work, at home and socially, and what aids and adaptations might be useful. They should also consider what special skills they might develop in such a situation. The different pairs then report back on their findings.

Disability and the institution

Participants are divided into small groups and asked to consider how the institution caters for people with disabilities by asking the following questions (it is important that the answers come from the participants rather than from the organisers):

- Is there a policy on disability?
- How are people with disabilities attracted to the institution?
- What programmes do they follow?
- Are they on special courses or integrated on mainstream courses?
- Are there any people with disabilities studying in their department?

Case studies

These can be adapted to relate to the experience of participants or to extend their experience as appropriate. In the following example participants are asked to read the case study and decide in groups:

1 What qualifications should Paramjit be aiming for?
2 What competences does she possess?
3 What evidence would there be to support them?
4 What issues might arise around her disability, particularly if she wishes to continue in education or training?

Case study

Paramjit Khan came to Britain when she was 13 years old. She comes from quite a wealthy family and received a good education in India before arriving in East London, where she attended a special school. She contracted polio when she was seven and is paralysed from the waist down. Paramjit left school at 16 with two CSEs and started attending a day centre, where she was unable to continue studying and did manual work such as packing for a local company until the work ran out.

Paramjit learned dressmaking from her mother, and also intricate embroidery. Her work was commissioned by a local shop and soon she and her mother were supplying tablecloths, cushion covers, scarves and other items to five outlets. She and her brother costed the work, bought material from wholesale outlets and took telephone orders.

Paramjit also became involved in a local Asian women's organisation. She was elected secretary, preparing agendas for meetings and organising events and speakers, as well as working closely with the treasurer to prepare the annual report. As the organisation had a grant from the local authority, she and the rest of the committee had to justify expenditure in order to secure more funds. Paramjit also taught embroidery to other women in the organisation.

Paramjit originally approached the college with the aim of improving her written English, but she would also like to obtain qualifications in some of the areas where she feels she has ability.

Information supplied by a college disability support team on NVQs and students with disabilities and learning difficulties

Issues

1 People with disabilities and learning difficulties experience the most problems in accessing vocational training.
2 Demographic changes mean that there are more employment oportunities for people with disabilities.
3 Lecturers and trainers need to shift their thinking in relation to the capacities and futures of people with disabilities.
4 NVQs open up access to those who may have been disadvantaged in the past, by giving recognition and credit for what they can do.

Further education should be pro-active in creating opportunities for this group of learners to achieve nationally recognised vocational qualifications.

General education's support role

The Disability and Learning Support Team can offer:

• Individual counselling and guidance to discuss support needs.
• Advice on individual learning plans.
• Advice on adaptions and aids.
• Relevant resources and equipment.

- Communicator support for hearing impaired students.
- Help and advice on the design of learning materials.
- Advice on various methods of assessment.
- Individual support for students with physical and sensory disabilities.
- Extra support for students with visual impairment.
- Staff development for course teams.
- Liaison with examining bodies over special exam arrangements.

Chapter 7

APL and women

A PICTURE OF UNDERACHIEVEMENT

Historically the experience of women shows a pattern of educational underachievement. Their employment outside the home tends to have been predominantly in low-status jobs often seen by them as a stop-gap, or in the kinds of work which emphasise service: that is, which draw on the skills and abilities traditionally associated with women's domestic roles. There is a continuing tendency to undervalue the experience women gain at home and at work, with a corresponding tendency in women themselves to devalue the skills and abilities they have acquired. Many women do use and develop their potential by returning to work, education or training, or by moving into more demanding areas of employment, but such moves are often fraught with difficulties. Equally, many women are demotivated in the world of employment as far as seeking training or qualifications is concerned. A study by Sanders, Fuller, and Lobley, *Emerging Issues in the Utilisation of NVQs*, Report No.5, found that female unskilled work operatives gave the following reasons for not seeking training or qualifications:

- lack of self-confidence
- low job expectations
- deference to husband's career
- anxiety about extra responsibility
- satisfaction with current job performance.

(Sanders, Fuller and Lobley 1990)

The problems women face in the workplace: discrimination, low pay, lack of childcare, limitations on job choice, inflexible working

© Lenny Peters

hours, and poor training, are constraints which impact upon women's occupational expectations.

Recognition of unpaid work experience

All the leading Examining and Validating Bodies have issued statements recognising that competences developed in the home and in voluntary unpaid work can, if they match the standard and performance criteria for qualifications, be accredited. However, as Linda Butler points out in her book *Unpaid Work* (Butler 1991), in the absence of any research into unpaid work competences in relation to job matching and recruitment, unpaid work can be stereotyped as limited in range of application and low-level, suggesting training and employment options which are limited and subordinate. In fact, skills and knowledge used in the home have been graded at NVQ Level 3 or higher by careers guidance workers using computer aided guidance, and include skills which clearly relate to employment, such as planning and supervising, as well as technical skills such as cooking.

Nevertheless, employers can deny any link between competences developed in the home and in paid employment, even though the boundaries between them are blurred by the fact that many people do paid work from home. The London Chamber of Commerce (LCC) draws attention to the fact that the incidence of paid work from home is likely to increase and that efforts to assess evidence arising from it for the purpose of obtaining a qualification should increase. The LCC statement recognises that the impact of modern technology will promote an increase in the number of employees working at home with a computer. More people will be home-based self-employed and there will be greater opportunities for women and people with disabilities to work from home.

Women's own low expectation of themselves can be an obstacle to change in this respect, and is often reinforced by those closest to them, who do not want to see them in their new roles.

The recognition of women's domestic experience for academic or vocational purposes is not new. Much of the publicity offering career guidance makes this plain. However, many Return to Learn and Access courses have concentrated on focusing on past achievements and experience primarily as a way of boosting personal confidence and gaining entry onto courses. In the

United States, however, it has long been possible to gain credit towards higher education qualifications for relevant experience.

In the UK, Access courses, which in general attract three women to every man, are based on the assumption that mature people who do not have the traditional entry qualifications for higher education may be able to benefit from it because of their previous life and work experience. Yet very few Access courses incorporate any APL which could enable students to gain credit for part of a course or even an entire course in certain cases. In contrast the Credit Accumulation and Transfer Scheme (CATS) operating in many higher education institutions has a generous policy for the recognition and crediting of domestic or other voluntary work, although in practice it is not much called upon to do so. Perhaps what these two facts illustrate is that both men and women have learned to perceive the experience gained in unpaid work as trivial and marginal in terms of its transferability to paid work or courses leading to qualifications.

If APL is going to be of real use in extending opportunities to women who obtain much of their experience in the unpaid and domestic spheres, then courses aimed at women must extend their remit and strategies to include ways of allowing accreditation of that experience, not just appreciation, important though this is. This aim fits in with the new funding structure for colleges whereby only schemes aimed at vocational qualifications will be financed. As mentioned previously, NCVQ have defined work as 'purposeful activity with critical outcomes' and although some of the range of statements of qualifications may limit the applicability of unpaid work achievement for gaining credit, the wide range of tasks performed outside paid employment, as identified by functional analysts, cannot be ignored. According to Linda Butler (Butler 1991) these include roles such as:

- financial management
- time management
- site supervision
- team building
- assessing
- buying
- catering
- tutoring.

At the moment, despite the policy statements on experience gained in unpaid work, there are not many examples of how and where it can be accredited. The core courses developed by the Examining and Validating Bodies have the potential for accrediting competences acquired in unpaid work. For example, the RSA Advanced Diploma in the Organisation of Community Groups allows evidence of competence gathered in the community and in voluntary work. In the future, when all City and Guilds courses will have Accreditation of Prior Achievement (APA) systems built in, for instance, opportunities are likely to increase.

APL FOR WOMEN

In their article 'Making Sense of Experiential Learning' in *Adults Learning*, Ian McGill and Susan Weil identify four types of APL or APA. The first type is concerned with the assessment and accrediting of experiential learning, whilst the other three emphasise different aspects of the intrinsic value of experiential learning in bringing about change in the individual, in society and in education (McGill and Weil 1989). The first type was seen primarily as maintaining the status quo. Perhaps because women's experience is different and undervalued, any APL offered has generally been found in the second, third and fourth types. However, the examples given show that it is possible to offer accreditation at the same time as ensuring that the women involved find APA or APL a positive experience, which will enhance their confidence and accredit their achievements and avoid confirming them in a low-status stereotyped role.

Models and principles

An access course

In general, although access students have the opportunity to consider their past achievements, most do not, however impressive those achievements, omit the access course and present themselves directly to the higher education institution for entry. This is due partly to structural reasons, since few access courses are modular and it is thus not possible to follow a quarter or half a course, which may be all an individual needs. At the same time few HE institutions admit students at any time other than October. However, the North East London Access Federation

(NELAF) has a policy of encouraging member institutions to offer a summer term programme to allow students interested in entering HE to assess their capabilities, analyse their past achievements and produce both a personal statement and a mini project. The personal statement is a detailed account of experience, future plans, and aspirations which could only be arrived at by considerable reflection. The mini project is an investigation, essay or product designed to give an indication of academic ability or to try out an area of study to test an interest.

The benefits of this period have been extensive. Some students have used their personal statement and mini project, together with a reference from their access tutors, to gain immediate entry into HE, and even to gain credit through CATS once there. Others have stayed on to complete an access year and gain a clearer idea of the direction they wished to choose. Others have decided that access was not for them and gone on to attend other courses in further education which they were not aware of before attending the summer programme. This programme has been of particular benefit to women, who are more likely, no matter how able, to lack the confidence to approach an HE institution. Many women joining summer programmes have turned to more vocational courses as being closer to their needs. Those who opted for HE have ended up with a much better idea of what they were letting themselves in for.

Access through independent study

Access courses can sometimes be accused of having too traditionalist a structure, an 'A' level curriculum without the 'A' levels. Notions of the importance of experiential learning, both off course and on, underpinned access courses at one college, and included the possibility of APL. At the start of each course students were asked to identify a topic, skill or problem which was of special interest to them. This then became the focus for their own individual and experiential programme of study. The students were encouraged to reflect on their learning experience as it occurred and in so doing to learn from it. They also engaged in a group project which they designed and implemented themselves, with the only proviso that each project require them to use study skills selected from the following categories:

- research
- communication
- numeracy and statistics.

Both individual and group learning programmes were divided into three stages:

1 Reflection and planning.
2 Implementation.
3 Presentation.

During Stage 1, the students explored, both individually and collectively, each student's prior learning experience, interests and expectations and, in the case of the group project, a burning local issue. The focus of the individual and group projects had to be expressed in terms of a number of aims supplemented by a description of methods. During Stage 2, the implementation stage, participants were required to identify a sequence of activities or tasks which needed to be completed if the aims were to be achieved. As tasks were carried out students had to reflect in tutorials on what had been learned and how learning had taken place. During Stage 3, the completion stage, the aims were matched against the achievements and the development of skills and knowledge was confirmed. This course structure emphasised prior learning experiences and empowered people to take control of their own on-course learning.

Learning Recognition Workshops

In an effort to attract on to mainstream courses women who had never attended college before and those who attended local adult education centre classes, a series of drop-in workshops in community centres was planned, and advertised in the press, libraries, social security offices, etc. The aims of the workshops were:

1 to generate self-awareness and a positive attitude to education amongst participants;
2 to determine whether students were at the right level for entry to college courses;
3 to provide career guidance;
4 to help participants to develop individual action plans in which to make their own decisions concerning where they want to go and what they want to study;

5   to accredit, wherever possible, prior learning for a vocational
    qualification or for academic purposes.

As well as individual interviews, considerable importance was
attached to the group work the students did, which helped them
overcome any shyness. First, the students were given an account
of Judith Jones's day. Judith Jones has a child and works as a
part-time secretary at the local secondary school. Her day is
described in detail and students have to identify the skills and
abilities she shows. (Judith's day is one of the case studies at the
end of this chapter, see p. 128.) They are usually surprised at how
many skills they can identify. This also gives the participants a
framework and language for analysing their own skills. The next
step is to get each person to analyse her own areas of skill and
knowledge with the aim of recognising and valuing such experience and abilities as she may have.

A number of exercises exist to achieve this. One is the lifeline,
where participants are asked to review the main experiences and
activities in their lives and then to identify skills and qualities.
Participants are then asked to pair off and start outlining the
experiences they have noted down. It will be obvious from some
of the participants' work that accreditation towards a vocational
award may well be a possibility. Others might be able to show,
through a collection of appropriate evidence, that they have
sufficient skills and abilities to be accepted on a course of their
choice. Others may simply be encouraged to look at a new area
for career progression. The process in the Learning Recognition
Workshop is illustrated in Figure 7.1.

For this system to work, a network of assessors in different
subject areas was needed, who were able and willing to assess
portfolios. Out of this need arose staff development to create such
assessors. Also needed was a breakdown of 'threshold competences' for courses students were likely to choose. Clear
statements of alternative competence-based entry criteria were
required for a spectrum of courses.

During the year the workshop was piloted five people went
forward to formal accreditation for Computer Literacy and
Information Technology (CLAIT) and for catering, three decided
to follow a BTEC First Computing course, and three auxiliary
nurses joined science access courses, with twenty-seven people in
all devising portfolios.

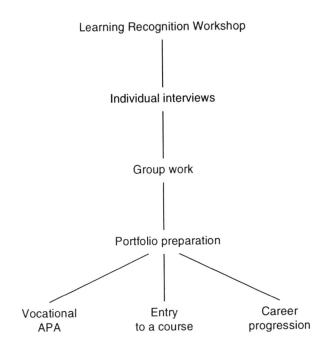

Figure 7.1 Learning Recognition Workshop process

Capability Assessment Programme

APL can also be useful for in-service training, to assess training needs. The APL unit in a large community college devised a Capability Assessment Programme for in-company use, designed to:

- provide employers with information on staff training needs
- raise the consciousness of employees concerning existing skills
- help employees draw up individual action plans
- accredit prior learning where possible.

The programme was initially set up in 1989 in response to a request from the local authority's Training Unit who discussed with the college how best to prepare for Compulsory Competitive Tendering. A pilot APL programme with town hall cleaners was established. These cleaners faced redundancy or retraining to fill clerical posts. The course was designed in two stages: the first deals with past and present experience and concentrates on identification of skills, knowledge and qualities with a view to enhancing individual self-confidence. The second stage focuses on identifying participants' future goals and exploration of strategies for achieving them.

All the participants felt that their skills and abilities as women were primarily those which centred around their roles as wives and mothers. They undervalued the skills they had acquired through the home. By the end of the programme they had not only drawn up a list of competences they already possessed but also perceived those which enabled them to operate effectively in the domestic sphere, e.g. problem solving, financial management, as transferable and of value in the field of employment. One participant had considerable skills in the clerical field and was able to match her skills with those stated in the ABC guidelines. Four of the other participants spent their time analysing the tasks they had had to carry out in previous jobs, which in one case involved carrying out reception duties, book-keeping and supervising staff. All of the participants felt some surprise at the amount and range of competences they possessed and felt more confident as a result. Three participants felt they required tuition to improve basic skills in literacy and numeracy. Two had recently attended an in-service workshop on Report Writing which they found depressing because they had poor writing skills, although their reading skills were adequate. They experienced relief that they could complete the Capability Programme with little or no writing. All identified clear goals for the future and training needs which were noted on the Individual Action Plans, some of which can be seen below.

All these programmes are in effect development techniques for initial assessment in a positive and supportive way which takes account of women's particular experiences. The programme was designed to generate an effective response to such questions as:

- what competences does the learner possess?
- what can the learner immediately demonstrate?
- what can the learner work to possess?
- what skills and knowledge does the learner need to update?
- in what areas is a training programme required to enable the learner to acquire the experience, knowledge and skills required for competence?

Return to Learn

The APL process can also be a learning process in itself, in a Return to Learn Programme, for example. In one case, a Return to Learn Programme had been established for many years, attracting a large number of Asian and black women to part-time day courses at Adult Education Institutes. The curriculum consisted mainly of basic skills tuition with vocational options. A pilot was set up to offer APL guidance and portfolio building. It became clear through this pilot that many skills and abilities had been overlooked by tutors. The very name of the programme seemed to suggest that nothing very valuable had happened in the time before the student had returned to learn in a formal context. The experience of portfolio building not only gave the students the option of attaining credit, but also became a valid educational experience. Portfolio development offered an opportunity to work on a broad range of skills in areas such as writing, reading and vocabulary building as well as helping students to examine the way they reason and analyse. Specifically, it is an opportunity for them to practise analytical skills in the context of prior learning, rather than writing about alien subject matter. Compiling a portfolio gave these students an opportunity to identify transfer skills they possessed, and to become aware of skills that could be developed. This approach helps students to define their strengths and weaknesses and provides a strong bridge between present skills and future choices of areas of study. Activities included:

1 using the portfolio as the major writing exercise;
2 giving students practice in narration, description, categorisation, argument and process;
3 working with students to identify academically transferable skills which they have developed throughout their lives;
4 assigning readings in areas where students had significant experiential learning. Asking students to compare and contrast information conveyed with knowledge they had gained through experience;
5 giving readings that analyse the same issues but reach different conclusions and asking students to evaluate the arguments offered in the light of experiential learning;
6 teaching research skills by familiarising students with library resources in areas of work and community experience.

At the end of the course students had practised English, communication skills, numerical skills and statistics and had often defined their own progression routes, as looking at the past made them clearer about the future.

This example illustrates how the introduction of APL can transform an existing programme and make it both more relevant to the needs of the students, and more closely linked to other available provision. This kind of link is a lifeline for women who have been isolated in the home, often in a strange country, and out of touch with the education system or the labour market, and demonstrates the role of APL in enabling the individual to find a role in society, in whatever area is most appropriate to her.

Staff development to introduce APL into this type of programme could consist of exercises with case studies, which can be devised to suit the group being trained and the candidates they are likely to come across. These should include people from different age groups and from different ethnic, linguistic and class backgrounds and those with disabilities or learning difficulties, so that counsellors are made aware of the applicability of APL to all candidates. Examples of case studies are given on the following pages, with a few sample questions to start people thinking about issues of accreditation. We conclude this chapter with the statements of the RSA and the NCVQ on the accreditation of achievement or competence gained in unpaid work. Although these statements do not specifically mention women they do both mention work in the home, as well as voluntary and community work. The recognition of work in the home as worthy of formal credit, as evidenced by the statements, does have very positive implications for women who have spent a substantial part of their lives running homes and bringing up families. However, the initiative lies with educational institutions to take up the issue and ensure that it is possible for women to gain access to the credits they have gained, and build on them to progress further.

CASE STUDY: A DAY IN THE LIFE OF JUDITH JONES

7.00a.m.   Gets up.
            Gets her seven-year-old daughter up and prepares her
            for school.
            Makes breakfast.
8.30 a.m.   Daughter collected for school by friend.

	Judith leaves for work.
8.45 a.m.	Arrives at work. Judith works as a part-time school secretary at the local secondary school. Her general duties involve dealing with mail, answering the telephone, servicing the headmistress Ms Dibb, and dealing with matters arising during the normal running of a school morning.
	Arrives to find one member of staff will be absent. Rearranges timetable and notifies other staff of revised teaching and room schedules.
	Today is the final day for collecting fees for the school educational holiday. She takes money, enters it and balances books. Makes arrangements to bank money on her way home from work.
	Fourth-former breaks his leg playing football. Sends for ambulance. Files accident report. Tries to contact mother but unable to reach her. Arranges for boy to be taken home by mother of boy's friend. Deals with headmistress's mail. Prepares coffee. Deals with query from prospective parents and arranges visit to school. Checks next day's diary with Ms Dib. Notes that a visit from a local councillor is due.
1.00 p.m.	Lunch break. Goes out for sandwich.
	Buys vegetables for supper.
	Collects dry cleaning and buys present for daughter to give friend.
2.00 p.m.	Returns to work.
	Answers query from local paper with regard to school play.
3.00 p.m.	Leaves work.
3.20 p.m.	Collects daughter Sally and friend Jemma from primary school (the other side of town). Takes them home for tea.
5.00 p.m.	Jemma's mother arrives, very upset. Wants to discuss her on-going marital problem.
5.15 p.m.	Judith's mother rings up: she has a hospital appointment next week – could Judith go with her? Mother obviously worried but friend in tears, so arranges to ring mother back.
6.00 p.m.	Husband arrives home. Jemma and her mother leave. Starts to prepare evening meal for husband.

7.00 p.m.   Evening meal.
7.30 p.m.   Tries to persuade daughter to leave television and go
to bed.
8.00 p.m.   Succeeds in sending daughter to bed.
Watches television. Discusses day's events with
husband.
11.30 p.m. Bed.

Worksheet: A day in the life of Judith Jones

Please discuss and work out together the main kinds of skill that
Judith shows in each episode.

Main skills

7.00 a.m.

8.45 a.m.

1.00 p.m.

2.00 p.m.

3.00 p.m.

5.00 p.m.

6.00 p.m.

11.30 p.m.

CASE STUDY: PAMELA CARTER

Pamela Carter is 22 years old. She left school in 1981, having obtained three CSEs in Home Economics, English and Biology and she had just failed her 'O' level Maths. She spent one year on an office skills course where she learned keyboard skills and did basic accounts. After being unemployed for a year she found work as a nanny in France, where she stayed for two years. She enjoyed the work and learned to speak French, although not write it, quite fluently, but had to leave when the children she cared for went to school. After looking for work for six months she obtained work as a nursery assistant in a local authority nursery. She was not very happy there as she was given mainly menial tasks, because she was regarded as a beginner. She left when she failed to get secondment to attend a NNEB course. She has been unemployed for fifteen months.

Pamela's interests include reading, dancing and playing computer games. She has a collection of games which she can amend by changing the program. She has a word-processor program which she has attempted to use and belongs to a personal computer lab. While she has been unemployed she has done some voluntary work helping in old people's homes and at the local hospital where she sometimes helps out at the reception desk.

She enjoys working with and meeting people but feels she is out of touch due to the length of time she has been unemployed and the fact that she has never worked in an office environment. She has decided that she no longer wishes to work with children and wants some sort of office work because it offers better pay prospects and 'less hassle' than nursery work. She is to be married in three months.

She expressed a particular interest in reception/typing work but feels that her written English might be a problem in anything but copy-typing work.

Read the case study and in groups decide:

1 Does Pamela possess any competences (skills, knowledge) achieved through her prior experience which may be of use to her?
2 What are Pamela's needs?
3 How could a Flexible Individualised Learning Programme help her?
4 How could this be organised?

CASE STUDY: MARY SMITH

Mary Smith worked for five years as an assistant cook in a large hospital. She started working in the hospital as a catering assistant and worked her way up to assistant cook, through on-job training and a number of short in-service training courses, all uncertificated. She also became a shop steward for her trade union, with specific responsibilities for dealing with day-to-day problems between line workers and the catering managers. She frequently had to explain one side's point of view to the other and if possible negotiate a compromise. If matters of employment law or union policy were involved, she had to consult the full-time official. Over time she became skilled in negotiating verbally with the manager and often brought about solutions acceptable to both sides in a dispute.

Three years ago, after an illness, Mary Smith was made redundant. She determined to make a living out of a hobby, and started, with a friend, catering for parties and other events and eventually built up a small, successful operation. She and her friend did all the cooking and administrative work such as accounts and ordering.

Despite this success, Mary Smith wanted a job where she could use her negotiation skills. She knew she was a successful union negotiator and could write clear concise reports, but her lack of formal qualifications discouraged her and she felt unsure of her ability to get a better job.

She had come to the college to see what options were available to her.

Read the case study in groups and decide:

1 What skills, abilities, knowledge, competences does Mary possess?
2 Could these be accredited?
3 Where, if Mary Smith came to your college, would she be directed?

NATIONAL COUNCIL FOR VOCATIONAL QUALIFICATIONS ACCREDITATION OF COMPETENCE GAINED IN UNPAID WORK

Recognition and development of competence is a major priority at this time. We need to increase skills levels and encourage many more young people and adults to grasp opportunities for education, training and qualification. This cannot be done if individuals and employers undervalue competence and if prior achievement goes unrecognised.

There are substantial numbers of people working in the home, in a voluntary capacity in the community, in voluntary organisations or in the uniformed services whose abilities and achievements are locked up, forgotten or go unrecognised. There are far too many people whose past experience is also overlooked. All this talent has been lost before, because there has been no adequate means of describing their achievements in a systematic, objective and meaningful way.

National Vocational Qualifications, and North of the Border, Scottish Vocational Qualifications now provide the means to do just that. Because they are relevant to work, and cover all occupational areas, they provide ways of recognising and giving credit for competence, wherever, whenever and however it has been achieved. The keys to this are the National Standards upon which NVQs and SVQs are based, and the method of assessment. This takes into account evidence from past as well as present performance, that national standards have been met. At last we have a system which makes it possible for *individuals* to take account of the full range of their experience, helps *employers* to build a full picture of the value of current and potential employees and enables *trainers and teachers* to provide flexible top-up courses to meet individual needs. The NVQ and SVQ frameworks are the maps which offer pathways for individuals to build on their past achievements and plan the direction and progression of their careers.

The National Council welcomes the commitment of the National Awarding Bodies to finding ways of recognising competence acquired in prior experiences or unpaid work within the NVQ framework. It commends the many initiatives which are the focus of this conference. This will, I am sure, open up opportunities for recognition and qualifications which will improve prospects for so many individuals who have not had a chance to progress before.

Sir Bryan Nicholson, CHAIRMAN

RSA POLICY STATEMENT – ACCREDITATION OF ACHIEVEMENT IN UNPAID WORK

The RSA Examinations Board believes that competence may be demonstrated during a variety of activities other than paid employment, including work undertaken in the home, in the community or for voluntary organisations. It is not necessary for individuals to undertake paid employment in order to qualify for access or to demonstrate their achievements.

This statement is consistent with the RSA's policy on equal opportunities and open access, which states that: 'the principle of open and equal opportunity for all is promoted in all areas of RSA's assessment activity (with an aim to overcome any inequality in relation to gender, race, religion, age and disability)'. It is also consistent with RSA's commitment to credit accumulation and transfer and accreditation of prior achievement, to ensure the maximum flexibility for the recognition of competence.

The Advanced Diploma in the Organisation of Community Groups is one RSA vocational qualification which has immediate relevancy to many people involved in unpaid work. It is a competence-based qualification and candidates provide proof of their achievements through the Cumulative Assessment Record and supporting evidence. This evidence may be drawn from any aspect of the candidate's experience, provided that it can be shown to be valid, reliable and authentic and the currency of the skills can be confirmed.

All of RSA's vocational qualifications lend themselves readily to the accreditation of achievement in unpaid work using the same system of assessment as that described above.

Centres that are particularly interested in developing this area of work are invited to contact Diana Farmer at RSA for further information.

Chapter 8

Issues of class

When looking at equality of opportunity issues related to APL for various sectors of the community in preceding chapters, the class factor has arisen in several contexts. The concept of class is obviously closely linked with level of education and qualifications. The dictionary defines middle class as meaning non-manual workers, and those people of working-class origin who obtain professional qualifications are generally considered to have changed class. In our introduction we saw that children of unskilled or semi-skilled manual workers have a more than 50 per cent chance of being unqualified themselves, and that a large proportion of unemployed people were previously employed in manual occupations. In Chapter 3 we saw that many young black people fail to achieve their full potential in the British education system, and do not gain the qualifications they are capable of gaining, and that immigrant communities such as the Bangladeshi community in East London include a high proportion of manual workers. The fact that having a disability or becoming disabled is more of a disadvantage if you are born into a working-class family, or are a manual worker, is mentioned in Chapter 6. Equally, a large number of women are employed in unskilled work or in domestic work in the home and do not seek training or qualifications through lack of self-confidence or deference to their husbands' careers (see Chapter 7). The British education system has perpetuated class divisions, in spite of the introduction of comprehensive schools, through maintaining distinctions between types of qualification and the values placed on those qualifications, in such a way as to channel young people along fixed routes at an early stage in their development.

© Lenny Peters

THE ACADEMIC/VOCATIONAL DIVIDE

Probably the key factor in keeping Britain well behind its European competitors in the education and training of its workforce is the traditional division between vocational and academic study, which is one of the main culprits in reinforcing class divisions. The majority of students in higher education still enter by the traditional route of 'A' levels taken in the sixth form, in spite of the opening up of other channels such as BTEC and access courses. At the same time commitment to vocational education and training in the UK is weak, and the incorporation of colleges under the Further Education Act is likely to lead to fewer rather than more 16- to 19-year-olds on courses, as colleges grapple with new finance systems and attempt to balance their books. However, NVQs and APL have the potential both to increase the number of working people with qualifications and to encourage more young people to enter education and training. An enquiry was set up in the London Borough of Newham to discover why only 10 per cent of pupils were going on to polytechnics and universities, a figure which placed it second from bottom in the UK. The report of its findings, *Higher Education for Newham* (Newham Council Education Committee 1989), concluded that three factors interconnected to produce this result:

- a low level of academic attainment
- a high level of social disadvantage, e.g. a high percentage of children living in poor housing conditions, in low socio-economic groups and in large families
- a lack of encouragement both in the early stages of the school system and from the family, community and local values which exist in East End society.

Parents and teachers alike were found to be pessimistic about young people's chances in HE; in fact many households were found to be hostile to any post-16 education or training. Some of the report's recommendations were that:

- pupils going directly into employment should aim to get into jobs where they could continue training
- pupils should be made aware of non-traditional routes to HE
- adults returning to study should have their prior experience and skills recognised.

One way in which APL can be used to improve this situation, which is not unique to London's East End, is illustrated by the following experiment. In 1992 the Department of Employment, through TVEI, funded a project on access to HE which focused on post-16 centres in Barking and Dagenham. This is an area where the recession is causing more young people to stay on in education although, in 1989–90, Barking had the lowest staying on rate in the country, with pupils traditionally leaving school at 16 to go into Fords, the docks or the printing industry. This project aimed to use APL to help students to recognise the skills and abilities they had already acquired, both inside and outside the classroom, and to increase the takeup of available progression routes to HE, including those through vocational courses. The work of the project consisted not only of using APL with students to prepare them for HE applications, but also of collaboration with HE institutions. Papers about the project were sent to the Academic Standards Committees of two universities. This resulted in agreements from admissions tutors to take into account the skills, abilities and knowledge presented by students from the project in their portfolios. In this way a first step was made towards the broadening of higher education admissions criteria to include experiential learning, as well as 'A' level, BTEC, NVQ and other vocational qualifications, which would indeed be a major advance towards bridging the academic/vocational divide. In addition, students who participated in the project said that it had made them think about higher education in a different way, and they recognised that previously they had tended to attach little importance to non-academic activities either inside or outside the school as far as their personal development was concerned. The project team recommended that: 'profiling and the assessment of informal as well as formal learning should be introduced more widely into the post-16 curriculum to enhance progression to higher education' (DoE 1992).

So the task of APL in this context is twofold: a change has to be brought about in the attitudes of young people towards their own achievements and possible progression routes. At the same time higher education institutions need to adapt their admissions criteria to include recognition of experience and skills gained outside formal education.

GNVQS AND APL

The introduction of GNVQs, in September 1992, theoretically constituted another bridge across the gap between academic and vocational education. By combining the three core skills of:

- communication
- application of number
- information technology.

with vocational competences, the qualification is designed to allow progression either to further and higher education or to employment and training. The basis for the assessment of the competences will be the same as for NVQs, so that APL will have just as important a role to play in the recognition of skills and abilities, and their matching to the appropriate competences. As far as the core skills are concerned, evidence of experience gained outside formal study may be particularly relevant, and all students will compile portfolios as part of the process of gaining GNVQs. Their recognition, by the Standing Conference on University Entrance, is of course crucial if GNVQs are not to prove yet another second-rate qualification, for university entrance purposes, less valued than 'A'level, in which case the old divisions will persist. The position of the NCVQ is that the credibility of GNVQs will depend on the quality of people coming through the programmes, but past experience might incline one to a certain scepticism in this respect. The FEU, in a discussion paper entitled *A Basis for Credit*, proposed the development of a post-16 credit accumulation and transfer framework to span all post-16 provision and qualifications, including AS/A levels, GCSEs, NVQs, GNVQs, BTEC, RSA, C and G, Open College Networks and degrees. The aim would be: 'to express credit in such a way that different routes and subject areas are accorded parity in terms of their value within the framework' (FEU 1992).

This framework would be based on *outcomes*, which are what the learner is expected to know, understand and do in order to achieve credit. The outcomes would be grouped in *units* which carry credit values, and the unit specification would include not only the assessment criteria and the awarding body, but also recommended prior study or experience, grading criteria, teaching and learning strategies, and guidance on APL and destinations and awards. If this kind of framework were to be developed it

would certainly go some way towards resolving the general confusion which seems to predominate at present within the British
education system and amongst employers.

It has been suggested by the Association of Vocational Colleges
International, in their report *Strategies for Vocational Education and
Training in Europe*, that what is missing in the UK is 'an over-
arching education and training strategy' and that there are no
'institutionalised "social partnership" mechanisms whereby industry, unions and educationalists come together with a precise
role for each of the partners' (Association of Vocational Colleges
International 1992). This, they suggest, accounts for the existing
situation of:

> a very low participation rate for 16- to 19-year-olds, lack of a
> broad base in craft-level qualifications, over-specialisation
> leading to an unadaptable workforce, and a narrow academic
> curriculum producing limited specialists too early, with insuf-
> ficient integration of the academic and the vocational.
>
> (ibid.)

Central to proposals for more integration between the academic
and the vocational, and to the expansion of vocational training is
the notion of credit for practical achievement rather than certification through formal examinations. These proposals, as embodied
in NVQs, GNVQs and the APL process have given birth to the
concept of competence, which in itself is not without problems.

The notion of competence

The development of widespread competence-based education and
training within a framework such as that proposed by the FEU
would theoretically open up opportunities not only for young
people, but also for all those over 19 who missed out on education
and went straight into employment, and for those whose jobs have
disappeared in the recession and who need to reassess their skills
and abilities in order to re-enter the job market. For all three of these
groups APL is a key factor in the process of redefining goals and
objectives, and evaluating what is needed to achieve them. However, the APL process itself needs to be accessible to people who are
not familiar with the jargon of education, and the notion of competence needs to be made clear both to candidates and to advisers
and assessors. The NCVQ developed the unit of competence

through functional analysis, and it is made up of a number of elements, each with its set of performance criteria. Obviously, these are necessary for the assessment of prior learning and enable candidates, as well as advisers and assessors, to match experience with the awarding of credit. However, two issues arise: one is the issue of language, which was discussed in Chapter 5, but it needs to be said here that language is an issue not only for candidates who are speakers of other languages, but also for people from working-class backgrounds, who may be put off the process when confronted with competences and criteria couched in indecipherable jargon. The other issue is the vast difference between competences, in terms both of the language in which they are expressed and the actual skills they involve. Compare the following, quoted by Peter Ashworth in his article 'Is "competence" good enough?' in the *NATFHE Journal*:

- The candidate is able to turn (carve) mushrooms.
- The candidate can apply methods and concepts of sociology to develop recommendations for organisational change.

(Ashworth 1990)

The second example would appear to lend itself far more to the possibility of subjective judgments being made than the first. It is also much more difficult to decide when a core competence has been adequately demonstrated than is the case for a vocational competence. In the case of communication, for example, a unit of City and Guilds Wordpower, which although not a recognised NVQ was designed to fit into the framework, stipulates that a person must communicate in an appropriate tone and at an appropriate volume. It is only too easy to imagine how these kinds of criteria could lead to discrimination against working-class candidates as well as speakers of other languages or those who are not familiar with the culture and customs of the UK. In Chapter 9 we will look at staff development for dealing with issues such as these, but a heavy onus remains with NCVQ, in developing GNVQs, in terms of ensuring that competences and criteria do not lead to discrimination. Peter Ashworth suggests that not only is some activity inappropriate for the competence model but that even some work-related activity is inappropriate. Yet one great advantage of NVQs for unskilled or semi-skilled workers is that they can be assessed and awarded in the workplace, without the candidate having to take time off or spend money on studying. Work Based Learning is another valuable strategy for developing a more qualified workforce and giving opportunities to those who missed out in the past.

Work Based Learning

The development of the Work Based Learning good practice model was initiated in 1981 by the Manpower Services Commission, the project management being transferred to the Further Education Staff College in 1984. The intention was to develop a new model for the delivery of vocational education and training to:

- assist workers and employers in responding to labour markets in which change is endemic; and
- provide a basis for the provision of continuous learning opportunities which such change implies.

(The Further Education Staff College 1989)

The idea was that workers and trainees should acquire new skills by using the workplace and their work role in an organised and planned manner and ultimately gain qualifications for what they had learnt. Work Based Learning is defined as: 'Linking learning to the work role' (Levy 1991).

It has three inter-related components, each of which provides an essential contribution to the learning by:

- structuring learning in the workplace
- providing appropriate on-job training/learning opportunities
- identifying and providing relevant off-job learning opportunities.

(The Further Education Staff College 1989)

Some examples, from the Work Based Learning Project, of how these three components can apply in different workplaces/learning situations, are given here and illustrate quite clearly how the three strands inter-react (The Further Education Staff College 1989).

Example 1: for a systems analyst/programmer working in the information technology division of a large finance house

Learning in the workplace

- Moving from working in a group involved in reviewing and improving existing software in use in the company, to a recently formed team developing software and implementing a new system to run on newly purchased hardware. *Intended outcome*: to gain experience of what it is like to implement *new* systems etc., rather than improve existing ones.

- After a suitable period, and in preparation for possible promotion, being given responsibility for training of junior programming staff. *Intended outcome*: gaining first experience of supervisory responsibility within company.

On-job training/learning

- Being allocated a set period of 2–3 hours each week to learn a new high-level computer language using manuals, and having the support of an experienced colleague if problems or queries arise. *Intended outcome*: competence in using the new computer language in various company projects.

Off-job learning

- Attending seminar run by external training organisation with expertise in financial management systems. This provides an opportunity to discuss, with outside experts, pressing implementation issues and problems associated with a current project. *Intended outcome*: identifying alternative options for completion of project.

Example 2: for a student pharmacy technician employed in a London teaching hospital

Learning in the workplace

- Working with staff in the dispensary who are unpacking supplies received, checking stocks of drugs held on the wards, updating computer records. *Intended outcome*: to build up a picture of how drugs are managed in the hospital.
- Working in out-patients in the associated non-teaching hospital in order to build up experience of working under pressure during clinic sessions. Learning how to catch up with routine tasks during quiet periods. *Intended outcome*: developing competence in managing a range of different activities.

- Working alongside experienced staff dealing directly with patients in order to observe how to communicate: using clear language, checking that each patient has understood instructions, not being patronising, etc. *Intended outcome*: to develop a range of communication skills.

On-job training/learning

- Being given specific instruction by an experienced worker on how to operate systems used in the hospital for drug control, correct procedures for handling prescriptions, etc. *Intended outcome*: competence in operating hospital systems and procedures for drug control, etc.
- Being shown how to clear the dot-matrix printer when jammed-up with sticky labels for drug containers; how to reload the continuous strip of labels into the printer; and how to decide if the equipment technician(s) need(s) to be called in if a serious jam occurs. *Intended outcome*: able to use the dot-matrix printer efficiently for typing labels for drug containers.

Off-job learning

- Day-release at an FE college for BTEC National Certificate in Pharmaceutical Sciences. *Intended outcome*: qualification to support competent performance as a pharmacy technician.

Example 3: for a communications and instrumentation field technician in the gas industry

Learning in the workplace

- Being called out by a supervisor to a field station to get experience of dealing with an unusual fault. The aim is to see what the problem consists of and to work with a more experienced technician to correct it.
- Working alongside an experienced worker supervising contractors' work in a field telemetry station (an installation which automatically collects data on various aspects of gas distribution and relays it by radio to a central control facility). The purpose of this is to get some first-hand experience of supervisory activities.

- Attending monthly 'problem clinic' sessions to share problems encountered during work activities with colleagues. These sessions are designed to help improve the effectiveness of the way technicians monitor equipment, diagnose faults and remedy them.

On-job training/learning

- Being given time to be shown how to use equipment-specific fault-finding algorithms by an experienced worker.
- Being given the opportunity to strip down a faulty sensor – which would normally be thrown away immediately – in order to see exactly what went wrong with it.

Off-job learning

- Attending day-release and evening classes in order to 'top up' qualifications with additional, specialist National Vocational Qualification units.
- Attending a short course, run by the manufacturer, on operating new automated diagnostic equipment for mobile VHF radio sets.

Example 4: for a full-time BTEC First Diploma in Science student on a work experience placement in the haematology department of a London teaching hospital

Learning in the workplace

- Spending days working in different sections in rotation in order to gain experience of auto-analysis for blood gases; electrophoresis of neonatal samples; record-keeping and computer operation.
- Working alongside different technicians in a support function in order to learn exactly what activities and responsibilities are involved in each technician's role.

On-job learning

- Visiting clinics to meet patients and observe consultants holding clinics in order to find out when and how samples are taken and how the results of tests are used.

- Learning health and safety guidelines through the support of an experienced worker, with a particular focus on sterile technique: avoiding cross-infection, minimising risk of infection from samples.
- Being shown, by an experienced worker, how to prepare and label slides, what to look for in normal and abnormal samples.
- Being shown, by an experienced worker, how to operate the auto-analyser; how to prepare and load samples, monitor operation of the machine, check results are within an acceptable range, despatch results to appropriate wards and to keep records within the department.

Off-job learning

- For this particular full-time student, the college-based BTEC First Diploma in Science was the major component of the learning programme and comprised a range of syllabus elements; it was ensured that there were clear links between these and the workplace activities.

Example 5: for a YT trainee bicycle mechanic employed in a four-person bicycle workshop/retail outlet, one in a chain of six specialist outlets

Learning in the workplace

- Working to a tight deadline, using manuals and specification sheets to decide how to fit an unusual, recently introduced headset bearing to an aluminium fat-tube mountain-bike frameset.
- Working with and observing an experienced worker size-up framesets for customers of different ages, gender and build, so that the bike they buy is safe and meets their requirements.
- Organising the schedule of repairs for a couple of weeks, to coincide with spares delivery, workshop time and customer requirements.

On-job training/learning

- Being 'shown the ropes' by an experienced worker regarding what to do to complete a quarterly stocktake.
- Being shown by an experienced worker how to get up to speed when aligning distorted wheels on a wheel-jig.

- Being assisted by an experienced worker to remove a seized handlebar stem for the first time, prior to being left to do one alone.

Off-job learning

- Attending a short, two-day course at head office on the new, computerised billing and stock control system which had just been implemented.
- Attending a day-release course on wheel-building at the local college.

The idea is not simply to provide a delivery mechanism for units of competence in NVQs but also to encourage individuals to take a much greater interest in their own development. An essential part of any work based learning activity is a reviewing process, involving collaboration between the learner, the workplace supervisor and the off-job trainer or college tutor. Throughout the learning activity the learner is encouraged to reflect on experiences, to look closely at his/her performance, to recognise skills used, and to identify strengths and weaknesses. Participants have the opportunity to reflect on what they have learnt and consider what further training or learning opportunities they wish to follow up. The initial basis of the work based learning activity for the participant is the Individual Development Plan (IDP), which has the following functions (The Further Education Staff College 1989):

- helping learners to become aware of their immediate and future learning needs
- ensuring that the learning programme designed for each learner genuinely meets his/her need
- involving the learner in the planning, monitoring and recording of his/her learning and achievement
- providing a record of agreement about the learning to be undertaken and the learning opportunities to be made available
- helping to establish and maintain coherence across and within the different learning opportunities provided
- providing a framework for discussion and decision-making about assessment and certification.

The drawing up of the IDP involves investigation and recognition of previous learning and achievement, so that Work Based Learning, while not being synonymous with APL, nevertheless incorporates the APL process and has many characteristics in common with it. The recognition of existing skills is a vital part of Work Based Learning because it facilitates the transfer of those skills to new situations. The recognition of competences previously gained at work makes it possible both to credit them towards NVQs and to identify further learning opportunities. The use of the workplace for assessment purposes makes it possible to accredit competences for which it would otherwise be difficult to provide evidence. As in the APL process, different methods of assessment can be used to evaluate and accredit Work Based Learning, including:

- traditional tests of knowledge and skill
- pre-determined assessment of specific performances
- assessment of performance during normal work activity.

As an example of the last of these, the following two reports were carried out by a lecturer on a part-time course leading to NVQs in Business Administration. The lecturer visited the workplaces of the candidates and through discussions with the employers and observation of the candidates at work was able to establish which units of the NVQs could be claimed.

Employer visit

Student	Manjula Patel
Employer	Dr Rajah
	London
Course	Business Administration – Part-time Day
Post	Doctor's receptionist
Date	4 February 1992
Time	4.30 p.m.

Dr Rajah confirmed that Manjula had been employed by him for four months from September to November 1991 as a full-time receptionist. Since January, she has been re-employed part-time for twenty hours a week. Dr Rajah said that Manjula was a good worker who could stay with the practice for as long as she wished. He said that there was the possibility of a full-time job in the future. Manjula's attendance and punctuality are good.

2.1   Dr Rajah stated that all the performance criteria were covered satisfactorily, including (e) because she sometimes makes calls to patients to give them the results of screenings and immunisations. However, he did express some doubts as to whether she could cope as effectively with mainly English speaking clients as much of her work involves using community languages. Underpinning skill (vi) is not covered as there is no answering machine.

2.2 The performance criteria are fully satisfied. Manjula's written English is fine.

2.3 The performance criteria are fully satisfied. Manjula often needs to use reference books and find information from patient lists.

3.3 The performance criteria are fully satisfied. Manjula does not, therefore, need to do this with an assessor.

5.1 The performance criteria are fully satisfied. Manjula looks after a stationery cupboard. She completes stock record forms and orders stock. She opens and checks deliveries and puts them in appropriate places. She will also check the cupboard each day and does a weekly inventory.

6.1 The performance criteria are fully satisfied. Manjula receives the post and separates personal from business letters. She then opens all the business letters, date stamps them and prioritises them. She follows procedures for receiving payments through the post.

6.2 Manjula very rarely despatches outgoing mail and Dr Rajah felt, therefore, that this was not really part of her job.

8.1 The performance criteria are fully satisfied. Dr Rajah also pointed out that Manjula had excellent non-verbal communication skills when dealing with people with language difficulties. She also works voluntarily in the temple dealing with public relations.

8.2 The performance criteria are fully satisfied.

9.1 All doctors' receptionists receive strict training in these matters. Manjula is aware of fire procedures and uses all equipment safely. She is responsible for checking gas and electricity before she leaves. The performance criteria are, therefore, fully satisfied. She is also being trained to administer urine tests and screening.

10.1 The performance criteria are fully satisfied. The two receptionists need to share the workload. She always passes on information and meets deadlines every Tuesday when work has to be collected by the Family Practitioners' Committee.

10.2 The performance criteria are fully satisfied. Manjula always greets regular clients by name and reports to Dr Rajah if she has any problems with patients.

12.1 The performance criteria are fully satisfied. She needs to file at least thirty to forty letters a day. The letters are all very important documents and filed numerically. She also keeps all the computerised records up-to-date.

13.1 The performance criteria are fully satisfied but I am unsure if use of only one software package is considered enough in the range of variables.

13.3 The performance criteria are fully satisfied.

14.1 The system has two parallel lines and an intercom but does not have a multiline.

15.1 There is no appointment system in the practice but apart from this all the performance criteria are fully satisfied.

15.2 Manjula keeps the reception area clean and tidy, although Dr Rajah will sometimes help her with notices and displays. I feel that the performance criteria are fully covered.

20.2 Manjula receives money for insurance forms which may be paid by cash or cheque. She follows procedures for keeping this money and keeping records of it. She does not, however, take credit cards. I feel, however, that the performance criteria are fully covered.

Manjula still needs to complete 2.4, 3.1 and 3.2 from Level 1. She may also need some more practice on telephone work in English. If she decides to take the admin. route, she will also need 11.2, 12.2, 13.2, 13.2, 14.2, 14.3 and 19.

Employer visit

Student	Winona Wright
Course	Business Administration Level 2 – Evening
Employer	Western Hospital
	London
Supervisor	B. Smith
	Unit Projects Manager
Date employed	Since June 1989

Winona acts as secretary and receptionist for a team of between three and seven people at various times. She is the point of contact for all visitors to the organisation and deals with people up to Managing Director level. She copes with an extremely varied workload. Winona's punctuality and attendance are both excellent according to Mr Smith. He said that she was the best secretary he had had in eighteen years. She is always prepared to do extra work, e.g. during lunch times if necessary. She is very capable of working on her own initiative.

Mr Smith and I went through the performance criteria for each unit and he gave details of those he believed Winona satisfied.

Unit 1   Winona sets up and uses both paper-based and computer filing systems in the department.

Unit 2   Winona takes all the incoming calls and also makes external calls on Mr Smith's behalf. She often has to take messages with detailed technical information. She also finds information when requested from the technical library and presents this to Mr Smith. She drafts letters of acknowledgement, processing and follow-up. She would draft her own memos when ordering stationery or confirming meetings.

Unit 3   Winona's typing skills are good. Her typing work varies from ordinary letters to detailed reports and technical documents. Her proof-reading skills are good and she has learnt many technical words from the building dictionary. She has been working on a database for the last fifteen months, inputting payment records, costing information and contractors' lists.

Unit 4   Winona has no experience of working with petty cash. For 4.2, however, she does check delivery notes against invoices and put in a job number. She checks three to four invoices a week for office supplies.

Unit 5   Winona is in charge of the stationery cupboard and decides when to re-order items. She checks deliveries and then puts them in the appropriate places. She will do an inventory of stock. Stock record cards and requisition forms are not used by the department.

Unit 6   Winona receives incoming mail. She also addresses all envelopes and sends mail out. She is responsible for taking mail to the postroom. The weighing and franking of mail is done by the postroom staff.

Unit 7   Winona does a great deal of photocopying. She can also take coloured copies using Letraset and collating and binding.

Unit 8   Winona gets on well with other members of staff. She can appear shy initially but Mr Smith feels this is because of her dedicated attitude to work. She avoids idle chit chat and time wasting. She is good at dealing with visitors to the firm.

Unit 9   Winona keeps an accident book and a First Aid kit in her office. She is aware of how to make reports to the Health and Safety Officer and use all the standard forms. Regular fire drills are also held to train staff.

Unit 10   Winona is good at working as part of a team with other members of staff. She has good relationships with clients of the company, contractors and technical reps.

Unit 12   Winona is responsible for all office files but the system in the department is not a complex one so more theory is needed for 12.1. Winona has been involved in putting reports together and working with a technician to decide on layout and presentation. She has also marked drawings and maintains the technical library. She therefore fulfils some of the criteria for 12.2.

Unit 13   Winona fulfils all the criteria for 13.1 and 13.3. In her previous post, she also worked on a spreadsheet program. Mr Smith said that the department had just installed Lotus 123 and would make sure that Winona got training on it to fulfil the criteria.

Unit 14   Winona uses a fax machine but does not fulfil all the criteria for 14.3.

Unit 15   Winona fulfils all the criteria for this unit.

Unit 16   Mr Smith said that Winona does a large amount of typing to a high standard in a short period of time. He believes that she fulfils all the criteria for this unit but it is difficult to tell without giving a test.

Unit 17   Mr Smith will speak to the person in the organisation for whom Winona did her audio typing work so that he can validate that it was done to required standards.

Unit 19   Winona sometimes arranges meetings within the organisation. She will arrange for the room to be available and send any other necessary information to the people taking part. She will also arrange for any resources to be available. She therefore fulfils all the criteria for 19.2.

Winona should now claim for 2.3, 2.4, 4.2, 9, 16, 17 and 19.2 in addition to those units and parts of units already claimed.

The Work Based Learning Project proposes an assessment map which allows for information to be entered by the learner as well as all those involved in training, teaching or supervising him/her at work.

Ideally, work based learning activities should be of benefit to employers as well as employees, in that they enable employees to function more efficiently and to develop their skills and abilities to meet the demands of the particular work role they occupy. However, not all workplaces have the resources or commitment to undertake the process satisfactorily, and precautions need to be taken to avoid negative experiences. Obviously, for work based learning activities to succeed they require considerable co-operation between employers, supervisors, trainers and tutors, and employees/trainees, and the necessary investment of time and resources needs to be made for planning, structuring, carrying out and recording the process. This is a more complicated undertaking than the APL process on its own, but with tremendous advantages for people who are working and for those for whom the best way to provide evidence towards accreditation is through work experience.

Work Based Learning can constitute a means of progressing from low paid unskilled work, without the major decisions and upheavals involved in returning to education in an institution-based form. For people who have grown up and who live in a culture which does not value education, for women living in a community which assigns them to domestic and family responsibilities first and foremost, the decision to undertake training or education is momentous and beset by difficulties. There is the expense involved. Even if fees are minimal, the cost of fares and materials can be a heavy burden for those on income support or unemployment benefit. For women (and sometimes men) there is often the problem of finding childcare, and also the issue of taking time away from domestic duties or from other caring responsibilities. With the decline of Adult Education Institutes and the emphasis on the recruitment of young people on to full-time vocational courses in further education colleges, that step into education or training is going to become more difficult for adults, and more people will be trapped in situations where they are not able to fulfil their potential and participate fully in society. Colleges will need to take an active part in promoting courses for adult returners and APL programmes, and to present them in a format which is comprehensible and easily accessible, with guidance workers/advisers who are familiar with the problems and situations the prospective candidates face. Otherwise the research and expertise which have gone into devising and developing these programmes will be wasted, in that they will not be reaching the section of the population which could most benefit from them, and the class divide will remain unchallenged.

Chapter 9

Conclusion

Some FE establishments have identified the APL process as central to their operation, recognising its function as spanning the period between an individual deciding to undertake a learning experience or obtain a qualification, and the start of the learning period. Such a definition of APL broadens it from a narrow service restricted to those students capable of obtaining full accreditation for NVQs, to an entitlement for all students.

Changes in the school system, with the National Curriculum and records of achievement, mean that people will become accustomed to the practice of learning being recorded throughout their lives, and will not expect to have to repeat learning already accomplished in order to gain accreditation. In spite of misgivings expressed by some higher education gatekeepers about the usefulness of GNVQs as an alternative to 'A' level, growing support for the NVQ movement does seem to herald a genuine possibility of breaking down the academic/vocational divide. Higher level NVQs are being developed, notionally up to degree and postgraduate level, so that the framework will eventually be complete from the starting-point of GCSE onwards. The idea of credits, the spread of CATS in HE institutions and the encouragement given to non-traditional entrants will mean that APL systems of some kind will have to be established and expanded.

Geoff Stanton, Chief Officer of the FEU, in 'The Contribution of FE Colleges in Delivering NVQs', in *Competence and Assessment*, has analysed the NCVQ framework and competence-based learning and reached the conclusion that it is so different from what has gone before that it will not be just a matter of retraining staff who work in the vocational educational and training systems, but that the systems themselves will have to be redesigned (Stanton 1989).

At the heart of this radical change is the fact that, previously, learners used to gain qualifications by passing courses, whereas in future it will not be necessary to have taken any course at all to be qualified. The survival of FE staff will therefore depend on their ability to offer:

- opportunities for work based learning
- access to assessment and accreditation
- diagnostic services – diagnoses of learning need, and the provision of flexible opportunities to meet them.

In this book we have pointed out and described some of the ways such services can be made available to the advantage of the whole community. Equality of opportunity depends crucially on access to accreditation; both physical access and access through the recognition of the varying cultural and educational backgrounds and wide ranging aspirations of members of different groups in our society.

Educational establishments will henceforth have to take account of the prior learning achievements of those they hope to attract, wherever and however those achievements have been accomplished. There are many institutional and external factors which will affect the type and range of APL available in any particular institution. The major institutional factors to consider if staff development in APL is to be implemented are:

- Is there movement towards competence-based assessment?
- Is there an institutional policy on APL?
- What assessment facilities exist?
- Are there flexible learning opportunities?
- What resources are available?
- Is there awarding body approval for APL in the institution?
- Is there a structure for APL?
- What will it cost?
- How will enrolment systems and administrative procedures be adapted?
- What are the equal opportunities implications?

Apart from structural changes, it is a prerequisite when introducing APL that those involved acknowledge the following basic assumptions:

1 People learn in a variety of contexts.

2 Knowledge and skills acquired by informal learning can be equal to those acquired by more traditional means.
3 Recognition of informal learning benefits individuals and institutions.
4 Economic performance will be enhanced and skill shortage lessened through a better qualified workforce.
5 Equality of opportunity will be enhanced.

Initial staff development should be aimed at increasing awareness of these intrinsic benefits. Many staff in educational establishments will have little or no experience of APL and many, having obtained their own qualifications through long years spent following courses, may look on it as a soft option. This chapter concludes with two initial exercises that could be used to introduce the concepts involved in APL.

EXERCISES

Awareness raising

This exercise centres around an account, originally written for a staff newspaper, of the week of an Adult Education Centre co-ordinator. Participants are asked to identify the competences shown by the co-ordinator. The exercise can be extended to show the difficulty of analysing experiential learning, by asking participants to divide the skills into different types under the headings:

- working with people
- working with things or knowledge
- working with ideas
- working with numbers.

The aim of the exercise is to get over the prejudice that nothing of value is learned through experience, by, first, showing other people's experience related to their own, and then by asking them to analyse the skills involved and write competences which are transferable to a different context. By doing this they will gain some understanding of the difficulty this presents to students, and the necessity of training counsellors/advisers to carry it out. Central to the discussion at this point will be the difficulty of finding the right language to describe skills and what is known, and of identifying skills in a variety of contexts.

A life in the week of an area co-ordinator

'What do you do?' I'm an area-co-ordinator for Community Edu-cation in North West Newham, based at Barclay Hall.' (I have to practise this, it's not a sentence which trips off the tongue.) 'Oh, Barclay Hall, that's evening classes isn't it?' 'Well, no, not just evening classes, we're open five days and five evenings, and then of course, there's the Outreach and East Ham and West Ham. And other centres and the voluntary sector.'

It's not easy to explain, so here's a snapshot week. I can use it as a handout when I get the 'what do you do' question. Or should I stick to the usual, 'I'm a teacher'?

Monday

Not really the start of a new week – there are the notes from Friday night – African dance was a huge success, but the drums were so loud the Yoga people threatened to walk out and the African dancers didn't leave until 10.15. What can we do? Re-jig class times, compromise, soothe. Into car, off to Waltham Forest College for validation to access courses. Meeting and college user unfriendly. Back to Barclay Hall for one of the Good Bits: teaching literacy. We're writing our own dictionary. This involves spelling, alphabetical order, organisation, and should keep us going for a few weeks. We've done 350 and there are only 39,650 to go.

Tuesday

No meetings planned for today. Let's get on with planning the summer courses, or how to satisfy the learning needs of people in Newham and the employment needs of part-time tutors with 'Is that all the hours I've got left?'

And I must get the minutes of the NW Network meeting out. We're trying to make sense of our combined experience on child-care, the different ways and different funding. You've got to start somewhere. Marlene is holding the fort in the office, all the phone calls, all the students dropping in for – well, it's probably what we 'professionals' call educational guidance and counselling – and she's doing the accounts, and making everyone who comes in feel good to be there.

First day for the Brian Didsbury Centre students to run the

canteen. They perform brilliantly, a real asset in striped aprons, hot toast and 'Can I bring it over to you?' They also want to come back next week. 'We like it here.'

No Stage 1 teachers' course tonight. It'll balance up next when I have to go to central London to do an observed teaching practice on a Welsh teacher. No end to bilinguality!

Wednesday

Catching up with admin; registers, pay claims, enrolments – which we are still doing. Have we go to 2,000 yet? Almost.

Talk to Frances about her work as a development worker with older adults. New areas every week, particularly discussed the 'invisible' older man. How many do you see around NCC?

International Women's Week this week – go to West Ham Town Hall to do a workshop on Older Women and Learning. We identify learning needs, as provider and consumer, have a good time, laugh and come away feeling ready for anything

Back to East Ham for Publicity, Marketing and Student Recruitment Sub-Committee. Adjust mind to formal structures but find it keeps slipping off. And I'm back on duty at 7 o'clock.

Wednesday evening

Discuss with ESOL teachers how we satisfy students who work full-time and have to learn English in the evenings, and, more difficult what about the students we are constantly turning away? No answers, of course.

Then I am quizzed by another student doing a project on ESOL provision in NCC. Suggest that this is more suitable for a PhD. I'm afraid a touch of exasperation did creep in.

Thursday

Bright and early to East Ham to engineers staff meeting to talk about how we can work to deliver 3 per cent of their curriculum offer away from East Ham Centre. Discussion a success (gold star, Bashir): problems, solutions, actions. We are getting there but it takes a lot of mind stretching to work out how parents with families can take in the thousands of pounds' training offers (with conditions) that employers are putting forward.

Back to base, briefly, before going to Forest Gate School for their inter-agency lunch – tea and coffee, bring your own sandwiches. Manage to identify source of funding to send creative writing students on a residential course. Thank you, Rotary. Shuttle back to Barclay Hall to make sure all seventy NW Network minutes are sent out (see Tuesday). On to East Ham – this is the second time today – for Community Education Directory Working Party. Thank goodness Jim Carter is doing this now.

Find out that I can miss the Lister School Community Council if I keep up with the minutes. I'll go next time.

Friday

Write an article for TC. Was it worth it? (Yes, Ed.) All part of the long haul to inform people in the college that there's life out there, and vice versa.

Another Good Bit this afternoon. Teaching access students. They're doing reports this week – I can listen.

If we were a really responsive college we'd be putting courses on at the weekend when people really want to learn! Sorry, I'm having my time off in lieu.

Marilyn Gabbitt, Area Co-ordinator, 1991

The use of evidence for APL

The aims of this exercise are to investigate what is involved in obtaining credit towards a qualification and to consider issues relating to using different types of evidence.

Participants are given a copy of the national competence standards for managers. They choose one element within a unit and answer the questions on the worksheet on the next page, then pass the worksheet to their partner and they discuss together whether the evidence offered is:

- valid
- reliable
- suitable
- authentic.

Language often comes up as an issue with this exercise, with lecturers who have performed the competences not understanding the wording.

NATIONAL COMPETENCE STANDARDS FOR MANAGERS

Sample units and elements

Unit 4: Monitor and control activities against budgets

Have you: *Tick*

1 authorised expenditure within agreed budgets?
2 monitored and controlled the use of resources?
3 monitored actual income and expenditure against projections?

Unit 8: Plan, allocate and evaluate the work carried out by teams and individuals

Have you: *Tick*

1 selected and devised work methods and activities to achieve organisational objectives?
2· set and updated work objectives with teams and individuals?

Unit 11: Exchange information to analyse problems and make decisions

Have you: *Tick*

1 led meetings and group discussions to analyse problems and make decisions?
2 contributed to discussions to analyse problems and make decisions?

Performance criteria

Unit 4 Element 4.1: Authorise expenditure within agreed budgets

4.1a   Prior to authorisation the implications of expenditure and any alternatives are assessed against specified criteria.
4.1b   Expenditure is within agreed limits, does not compromise future spending requirements and conforms to the organisation's policy and procedures.

4.1c   Requests for expenditure outside the managers' responsibility are referred promptly to the appropriate people.

4.1d   Where appropriate, expenditure is phased in accordance with a planned time scale.

Unit 4 Element 4.2: Monitor and control use of resources

4.2a   Recommendations for improving the efficiency of operations are passed on to the appropriate people with minimum delay.

4.2b   Information on costs and resource utilisation is fully assessed, correctly interpreted and effective action taken.

4.2c   Prompt corrective action is taken in response to significant deviations from predetermined standards.

4.2d   Additional information is requested, where necessary, to improve decision-making.

Unit 4 Element 4.3: Monitor actual income and expenditure against projections

4.3a   Actual income and expenditure is checked against agreed budgets at regular, appropriate intervals.

4.3b   Where a budget shortfall is likely to occur, the appropriate people are informed with minimum delay.

4.3c   Any necessary authority for changes in allocation between budget heads is obtained in advance of requirement.

4.3d   When necessary, expenditure is rescheduled in order to maximise benefits.

4.3e   Any modifications to agreed budgets during the accounting period are consistent in advance of requirement.

4.3f   Prompt, corrective action is taken where necessary in response to significant deviations from budget.

Unit 8 Element 8.1: Select and devise work methods and activities to achieve organisational objectives

8.1a   Work methods and activities conform to legal and organisational requirements and are consistent with agreed staff working conditions.

8.1b   Work methods and activities are consistent with current management priorities and organisational objectives.

8.1c   Work methods and activities optimise the use of available material, capital and human resources within existing constraints.

8.1d   Where legal and organisational requirements conflict, the problem is identified and advice is sought from the appropriate personnel.

8.1e   Calculations are of a type and accuracy appropriate to the scale and importance of the work being planned.

Unit 8 Element 8.2: Set and update work objectives with teams and individuals

8.2a   Objectives are clear, accurate and contain all relevant details.

8.2b   Achievement of the objectives is practicable within the set period given other work commitments.

8.2c   Objectives are explained in sufficient detail and in a manner, level and pace appropriate to the relevant individuals.

8.2d   Objectives are updated regularly with the relevant individuals to take into account individual and organisational changes.

8.2e   Evaluation of the applicability and appropriateness of objectives for individuals is used to improve future objective-setting.

Unit 11 Element 11.1: Lead meetings and group discussions to analyse problems and make decisions

11.1a   The purpose of the meeting is clearly established with other group members at the outset.

11.1b   Information and summaries are presented clearly, at an appropriate time.

11.1c   Positive contributions and useful information which help decision-making are encouarged from all members of the group.

11.1d   Members are encouraged to be positive about the group.

11.1e   Unhelpful arguments and digressions are effectively discouraged.

11.1f   Discussion time is allocated to topics according to their importance, urgency and complexity.

11.1g   The leadership style is appropriate for the purpose and membership of the group.

11.1h Any decisions taken fall within the group's authority.
11.1i Decisions are recorded accurately and passed on as necessary to the appropriate people.

Unit 11 Element 11.2: Contribute to discussions to analyse problems and make decisions

11.2a Preparation is sufficient to make a useful contribution to the discussion.
11.2b Own contributions are clear, accurate and timely.
11.2c Contributions and viewpoints from others are discussed constructively.
11.2d Any appropriate section/departmental views are represented effectively.
11.2e Own contributions are directed at clarifying problems and identifying and assessing solutions.

Management competences – Self-assessment exercise

Element chosen:

1 Relevant experiences:

Within the last year . . . .

. . . .

. . . .

. . . .

Within the last two to five years . . . .

. . . .

. . . .

. . . .

More than five years ago . . . .

. . . .

. . . .

. . . .

. . . .

2 Possible evidence:

· ·

· ·

· ·

· ·

· ·

· ·

· ·

3 Other methods by which you could demonstrate this competence:

· ·

· ·

· ·

· ·

Both these exercises aim to familiarise staff with the concepts of APL through looking at their own experience before considering their application to the experience of others.

Although APL is important within formally accredited systems, to ensure equality of opportunity it is equally important that there should be institutional commitment to offer APL to all adult learners, both inside and outside such systems. APL is of value to learners and institutions even though the process may not lead to accreditation, because, as we have tried to show, APL addresses the needs of adult learners and is part of a strategy to widen access to education for all learners. It can provide a structure that will attract adults who would otherwise remain outside the life of an educational establishment. If colleges and universities are to fulfil their missions to become resources accessible to all members of their local communities, then APL has to be conceived as an integral part of an institutional strategy to widen access to learning opportunities and, therefore, create genuine equality in education.

References

CHAPTER 1

Barnes, C. (1992) 'Civil Rights and Wrongs', *Guardian* 11 March.
Central Statistical Office (1992) *Social Trends 22*, London: HMSO.
Department of Education and Science, Department of Employment, Welsh Office (1991) *Education and Training for the 21st Century*, London: HMSO.

CHAPTER 2

City and Guilds of London Institute (1991) *City and Guilds Equal Opportunities Statement*, London.
CNAA (1989) *Regulations, Credit Accumulation and Transfer Scheme*, 2nd ed., London.
NCVQ (1988) *Access and Equal Opportunities in Relation to National Vocational Qualifications*, London.

CHAPTER 3

Andrews, M. (1992) *Access and Staff Development Project*, London: Birkbeck College and TEED.
Bird, J., Wan Ching Yee and Myler, A. (1992) *Widening Access to Higher Education for Black People*, Bristol Polytechnic and Employment Department.
FEU (1987) *FE in Black and White*, London: Longman for FEU.
Lago, C. and Ball, R. (1983) 'Helping in a Multi-cultural Context', in *Multiracial Education* II (2).
McKelvey, C. and Peters, H. (1991) 'Language and NVQs', in *Adults Learning* 3 (3).
Mukherjee, M. (ed.) (1984) *Breaking the Silence: Writing by Asian Women*, London: Centerprise Publishing Project.
Nicholls, S. and Hoadley-Maidment, E. (eds) (1988) *Current Issues in Teaching English as a Second Language to Adults*, London: Edward Arnold.

Robson, M. (1988) *Language, Learning and Race*, London: Longman for FEU.

Wilson, A. (1978) *Finding a Voice: Asian women in Britain*, London: Virago.

UDACE (1991) *What Can Graduates Do?* A Consultative Paper, Leicester.

UDACE (1992) *Learning Outcomes in Higher Education*, Leicester.

CHAPTER 4

National Academic Recognition Information Centre (1991) *The International Guide to Qualifications in Education*, London: Mansell.

World University Service (1990) *Recognition of Overseas Qualifications: Doctors Professional Requalification: Lawyers*, London.

CHAPTER 5

Chanda, N. (1990) 'Assessment of Prior Learning: A Commonsense Approach for ABE and ESOL', *ALBSU News* 37.

FEU/NATECLA (1989) *Language in Education*, FEU.

ILEA (1990) 'Afro-Caribbean Language and Literacy Project in Further and Adult Education 1990', *Language and Power*, London: Harcourt Brace Jovanovich Ltd.

NCVQ (1988) *Access and Equal Opportunities in Relation to National Vocational Qualifications*, London.

Romaine, S. (1989) *Bilingualism*, Oxford: Blackwell.

CHAPTER 6

Barnes, C. (1992) *Disabled People in Britain and Discrimination: A Case for Anti-discriminatory Legislation*, British Council of Organisations of Disabled People, London.

Hanna, L. (1992) 'Leaving the Able-bodied Standing', *Guardian* 10 April.

Mason, M. (1992) 'The Disability Movement', in *Disability Equality in the Classroom: A Human Rights Issue*, Disability Equality in Education.

NCVQ (1988) *Access and Equal Opportunities in Relation to National Vocational Qualifications*, London.

Open University *Guidelines on Dyslexia*, Milton Keynes.

Rieser, R. (1992) 'The Language we Use', in *Disability Equality in the Classroom: A Human Rights Issue*, Disability Equality in Education.

CHAPTER 7

Butler, L. (1991) *Unpaid Work*, Learning from Experience Trust.

McGill, I. and Weil, S.W. (eds) (1989) 'Making Sense of Experiential Learning: Diversity in Theory and Practice', *Adults Learning* (1), January.

Sanders, M., Fuller, A. and Lobley, D. (1990) *Emerging Issues in the Utilisation of NVQs*, NCVQ Research Report, 5.

CHAPTER 8

Ashworth, P. (1990) 'Is Competence Good Enough?', *NATFHE Journal*, December.

Association of Vocational Colleges International (1992) *Strategies for Vocational Education and Training* 4, London.

FEU (1989) *Work Based Learning Project*, London.

FEU (1992) *A Basis for Credit*, London.

Further Education Staff College (1989) *A Guide to Work Based Learning Terms*, Bristol.

Levy, M. (1991) *Work Based Learning: a Good Practice Model*, Bristol, The Staff College.

Newham Council Education Committee (1989) *Higher Education for Newham – Report of the Inquiry chaired by Professor Peter Toyne*, London.

South Bank Polytechnic (1992) 'The Assessment of Prior Learning, Progression and Skills for Science' *Report of the BP Access Project*, London.

Staff College (1992) *Strategies for Structuring Learning Opportunities in the Workplace and Implementing Work Based Learning*, Bristol.

CHAPTER 9

Stanton, G. (1989) 'The Contribution of Further Education Colleges to Delivering NVQs', *Competence and Assessment* 9.

Index